# OPEN LAND IN URBAN ILLINOIS

*Roles of the Citizen Advocate*

# OPEN LAND IN URBAN ILLINOIS

*Roles of the Citizen Advocate*

*by*

**Rutherford H. Platt**

*Foreword by*

Paul H. Douglas

Northern Illinois University Press

*DeKalb, Illinois*

*The clothbound edition of this book is limited to 500 copies.*

*International Standard Book Number 0–87580–021–1*

Rutherford H. Platt is staff attorney for the Open Lands Project, Chicago.

Ours is not a massive, or a dramatic landscape. Contours are scarce.
Its values are in the textures, the colors, the variety, the intimacy,
the lustiness of the hardwood forest on fertile soil.
Further, there is in their spaciousness even grandeur in our meadows.
Punctuating the whole are the sharp and definite changes of our four seasons

*Charles "Cap" Sauers (1893–1970)*
*Superintendent*
*Cook County Forest Preserve District*
*1929–1964*

# CONTENTS

# ILLUSTRATIONS

Maps by J. Piccinini

## FOREWORD

This book seeks to interest individuals in protecting the environment either as landowners or as apartment and house dwellers. Rutherford H. Platt shows from a number of specific instances how one can become a "land advocate"—sometimes at a minimum of financial cost but always with great emotional satisfaction.

The economic stimulus comes from the tax system. A gift of land to a non-profit-making body will enable the owner to deduct annually up to 30 percent of his gross income. In the illustration chosen by the author in chapter three, a man with a gross income of $40,000 a year will therefore have his income taxes remitted on $12,000 of this. This, according to his computations will, for a "normal" family, save $5800. If the land had a market value of $72,000, he could charge off $12,000 a year for six years and thus save $34,800 in income taxes. Moreover, in his illustration, which assumes an original purchase price of $12,000, the maximum capital gains tax on the $60,000 profit (if sold) would be 25 percent; donating the land would save $15,000 more. This would make his total tax savings $49,800, or slightly over four times the original price paid for the land. While his gains would have been slightly less than if he had sold to a private holder, they would not have been greatly so.

In addition, the donor would have the solid satisfaction of giving green space for a growing population and of winning public esteem as a philanthropist. These are strong inducements. They are having some effect in the Chicago area as land taxes steadily mount on farm land, unaccompanied by any corresponding increase in agricultural revenue. The Open Lands Project deserves great credit for inducing gifts of such land. The chief hope of this transfer lies, however, in large-scale public purchase. But this is costly as land values increase and, moreover, voters tend to shrink from accumulating more public debt, and referenda are likely to lose as a consequence.

Voters need to realize the role of trees and grass in reducing the pollution of the atmosphere. City life multiplies the poisons discharged into the air and causes the steady increase in the deadly oxides of carbon. These can partially be controlled at the point of emission, and far more can be done in this direction. Reducing the waste cast off by the internal combustion engine in automobiles and using non- or low-sulphurous fuels to generate power and heat are important steps. And I see no more effective way of doing this than by public inducement or, if necessary, regulation.

But more can also be done by not decreasing and, if possible, actually increasing the supply of oxygen, roughly 70 percent of which is produced, as botanists and micro-biologists tell us, by the plankton of the sea, and 30 percent by the trees and grass of the land. As population increases and cities and suburbs grow, these sources of oxygen decrease and are replaced by buildings and more concrete, which are organically dead. Society thereby loses the marvelous regenerative power of living green things. For trees and grass absorb and separate the poisonous oxides of carbon, taking out the carbon to create both a source of nutriment and growth to the vegetable organism, and purified oxygen for the environment.

Urban civilization has weakened and largely destroyed these naturally recuperative powers of nature. The famous architect and city planner, Le Corbusier, not knowing this, did a great disservice in advocating a geometrical city in which trees were non-existent. I well remember the famous Chicago architect who, thirty years ago, denounced me for daring to plant trees in the ward in which I had been elected alderman. Indicative of the power of wrong ideas to survive if they are only advanced by the "right" people, I met an eminent city planner and disciple of Le Corbusier who recently refused to plant a tree in front of his New York house because "trees were not meant for cities." (Both of these men, incidentally, spent most of the year in the countryside on beautiful estates filled with the trees that their policies would have deprived the lower-income residents of the inner city from enjoying.) Trees also lower the temperature. Suburbs are cooler than the cities and the country cooler than the suburbs. Coolest of all are the forests and parks. Is it too much to hope that the intellectuals will recover from their love affair with Le Corbusier? Let it be clear that these once fashionable ideas are supremely wrong and that trees and grass are the most effective local purifiers of the atmosphere and, at least to some extent, the soul.

But trees are things of beauty as well as engines of purification. The more of them that city dwellers can see and live with, the better will be their lives. What would New York be like without its Central Park, Boston its historic Commons, and Chicago its chain of parks and Forest Preserve? Yet all of these cities have far less park space than London, Berlin and Paris each have—and they suffer in consequence.

In this country, two 17th century founders of cities tried to preserve a rural setting for their creations: General Oglethorpe, in laying out Savannah; and the Quaker, William Penn, in planning

Philadelphia, his city of brotherly love, where he tried to provide special civic places and quiet recreation. Penn's city was located between the Delaware and Schuylkill rivers. Dividing it into quarters, he fixed at its center a square that could include both a town hall and a park. It was here that his two main thoroughfares intersected. One ran north and south, the other east and west, and at the center of each of the four quarters he placed another park.

In view of later developments, which Penn could not foresee, his city plan proved grossly inadequate for the 20th century and even for the latter part of the 19th. The unprecedented growth in population, the development of high rise apartments, and the spread after the Civil War of the ugly red-brick two-story individual houses all combined to disfigure the city and to make it for half a century one of the least attractive large cities of the world. But for the 18th and early 19th centuries it was a model. It was saved by two developments. It was the site of the Centennial Exposition of 1876 which, though meant to celebrate the development of mechanical power, brought into being the lovely and gracious Fairmount Park. Then, in our day, the Philadelphia Plan came into existence. It gradually was accepted by the community; the Pennsylvania Railroad shifted its main station from opposite city hall to the banks of the Schuylkill, and then electrified its lines. Under the stimulus of urban renewal backed with federal aid, the city then carried out a gigantic program centering on the area around Independence Hall where the Republic had quite literally come into being.

Philadelphia has also experimented with transforming some of the lots on which abandoned houses rested into small block flower gardens and play areas. This has made it possible for very small local groups to take part in planning, setting up and maintaining these new lots. The city furnished fertile soil, some fertilizer, a share of the seed and some water. The residents provided primarily labor and care, with a small contribution of money so that they might feel that they were participants. I remember one block in particular, where a flower garden was planted one year and a play lot created the next. The members of the block then decided to plant and display large red flowers outside their front windows. What had been a hideous dilapidated slum only three years before was transformed into a beautiful neighborhood. Families were keeping their houses clean and repairing and painting them. Block behavior had so improved that flowers were appearing in the next block.

These are some of the ways in which families who ordinarily regard themselves as helpless can cooperate under skilled and sympathetic leadership to bring back a touch of nature into the drab streets of our cities.

But there needs to be built up from these and a host of other sources a coalition devoted to the saving of our land. Sections of such a coalition are already in existence and at work. The Sierra Club, the Wilderness Society, and the Izaak Walton League are gaining strength and becoming increasingly concerned. In our own area, Illinois and Indiana, the Open Lands Project and the Save the Dunes Council have prevented the worst from happening and have launched effective counter movements. Individual philanthropists like William Rutherford of Peoria, and the Rockefeller family have been of enormous help. All classes can help, for all stand to gain: the rich as well as the poor and the middle class, the black as well as the white, the conservatives as well as the liberals. All can work in comparative harmony upon different aspects of the common problem. There is enough work for everyone. But the numbers in the ranks of the public interests are still too few and their resources too scanty to meet the needs of the nation and the locality. The problem for the future is whether enough new recruits will come forward to man the ranks. Thanks to the author, this informed and moderate little book should help to educate the general public and to inform the soldiers of the help they may need.

Paul H. Douglas

# PREFACE

How does the writing of a book begin? This one never did. It is the result of the sedimentary deposition of unfinished lesser projects. Perhaps the more cogent question is how does the writing of a book end? This one just did. The subject is too timely, too dynamic ever to reach a satisfactory conclusion.

Two years ago I joined the Open Lands Project as a part-time staff member while I studied for the bar exam. My original assignment was to write a pamphlet on land donations, with special emphasis on the Chicago Metropolitan Area. Inspired on the one hand by the literate exposition of "stewardship" by Charles Little of our New York sister organization, and on the other hand by the careful legal analysis of Allison Dunham, my former professor at the University of Chicago Law School, my initial goal was to synthesize these two approaches.

The "pamphlet" grew as I decided to include a badly-needed citizen's guide to governmental activities in the open space field. It grew further as my geographical self demanded a physiographic view of the land around Chicago, not to mention some preliminary information on urban sprawl and population to set the stage.

After I had joined the Open Lands Project as full-time staff attorney, I soon realized that the "big story" lay right on my desk and in the office files. Under its Executive Director, Gunnar A. Peterson, the Project during its five years of existence had developed a unique style and rapport with the vast urban region which it served. Direct personal contacts with private citizens, with public officials, with conservation specialists and with the Loop "Establishment," made possible an extraordinary network of environmental communication. Under the aegis of this network, grassroots citizen groups in all corners of the metropolitan area fought their individual campaigns. While the obstacles and opportunities varied from one case to another, all at least knew that others fought the same fight. Through mutual reassurance and profiting from each other's mistakes, the practice of "land advocacy" in Chicagoland has begun to take on the semblance of an art. This book, as now completed, is a summary of the state of this art.

I am indebted to the Open Lands Project Board of Directors, and its President, Jeffrey R. Short, Jr., for allowing me to write this book on "company time." In particular, Gunnar Peterson has encouraged and supported my constant enlargement of the opus without demanding the results by a fixed deadline. I appreciate the critical reading of the manuscript by George W. Overton and Walter Fisher of our Board, and later by William H. Whyte.

The office staff at the Open Lands Project has lived with this manuscript far too long—Lynne Guth, Helen Smith, Susan Burnam, and Peggy Johnson have all labored over the keys on its behalf.

Finally, to the "land advocates" themselves, I say thank you for doing what you did.

R.H.P.

November, 1970

## INTRODUCTION

The Land is America's premier resource. It was the magnet which attracted colonists and immigrants from more crowded, used-up continents. It has been the source of America's agricultural wealth, its abundance of mineral resources, and its plenitude of living space. No wonder Americans have long taken their land for granted.

The land, however, is not infinite in supply and is capable of being destroyed, or at least permanently altered in character. It may be leached, eroded, blighted, polluted, desiccated, flooded, carted away, or encased in cement. Under the auspices of urban development, land is subjected to all of these insults. The result is an urban landscape teeming with humanity but ecologically more barren than a desert.

The urban desert, however, is not without its oases. Public parks, private back yards, regional forest preserves, and pockets of unspoiled plant communities provide many benefits to the landless urban populace. Depending on their size, location, character, and ownership, such pieces of open land may help to refresh the common air, to protect natural drainage and flood run-off channels, replenish underground aquifers, provide refuge to native flora and fauna, and afford scenic views and recreation opportunities to members of the public.

Such oases of functional open space do not exist accidentally. Deliberate public or private action is required to spare them from the remorseless tide of development. Otherwise, fertile soil, stands of oak, primordial bogs, and significant topography may all be sacrificed to the demands of construction and "progress." Like a masterpiece of art, once the open land is destroyed it cannot be replaced. To borrow the title of William H. Whyte's latest book, we are fast using up our "last landscape."

The development process is by no means a monolithic steamroller. Rather, it is a composite of individual decisions made by thousands of participants with the usually worthwhile objective of providing homes, jobs, and transportation, and fulfilling other needs. Seldom, however, do their objectives include the provision of open land which basically does not make money. Only the most sophisticated builders recognize that this provision can make *other* land more valuable.

Governmental bodies have made some heroic efforts to retain open land in the face of urban sprawl—the Cook County Forest Preserves are a case in point. The newer the suburb, however, the less effective the public lands program. Schools and roads compete for the tax dollar, and misunderstanding as to the benefits of open land impedes decisive action.

The burden therefore has fallen in many cases to the concerned private citizen to ensure that his metropolitan habitat does not lose its life-giving oases of open spaces. Land owners as "stewards to posterity" can effectively protect characteristics of their own land worth saving, while enjoying financial benefits in the bargain. Residents of developing areas, who do not actually own the land in question, may be effective in persuading the owner and/or public officials to protect necessary open land.

The owner as "land steward" and the informed citizen as "land advocate" are thus key participants in the urban development process. Their efforts are always individualistic and usually unsung. Seldom is their experience recorded for the benefit of others in like position and for the scholar of urban development. This book endeavors to provide such a record.

*Figure 1. Burnham's 1909 Plan of Chicago, showing lakefront parks, inland regional parks and boulevards, and proposed forest preserves.*

# 1
## THE METROPOLITAN CONDITION

In the United States there is more space where nobody is than where anybody is.
This is what makes America what it is.

To most people Gertrude Stein's descriptive definition may seem as accurate today as when she wrote it in 1936.[1] Why be alarmed about the supply of open space? Most of the United States is still undeveloped. All of our cities, roads and railroads combined occupy only 4 percent of the land area. Even our farms and ranches together cover less than half of the country. We still have vast, sparsely inhabited regions in the Great Plains, the Rocky Mountains, the deserts of the Southwest, and the backwoods of Maine, not to mention the far reaches of Alaska. Even if our metropolitan areas were to expand at the rate of a million acres a year, we would be centuries away from the radical land shortage experienced by Japan, the Netherlands, and Great Britain. A coast-to-coast flight on a clear day tends to convince most airline passengers that there is no cause for panic about dwindling open spaces.

But uninterpreted facts sometimes mask realities. The truth is that most of us, most of the time, simply do not live in the land of "purple mountains' majesty" or "the big sky." More than 60 percent of us reside today in or within commuting distance of the city. Reliable projections indicate that this proportion will climb to 71 percent in 1985 and 77 percent in the year 2000. The Urban Land Institute forecasts that in the latter year, 239 million people will live in urban complexes comprising 11 percent of our land.[2] Three decades from today, in other words, many more people than now inhabit the entire country will live in urban regions three times the size of present metropolitan areas.

There is little hope that this trend could be significantly retarded, much less reversed, even if it were deemed desirable. In our industrial-commercial-technological society, only cities can provide the significant employment opportunities of the future. One must live within tolerable reach of one's job, and that narrows it down to a choice within the metropolitan area. No matter where the teeming millions might prefer to live, that is where they will be. It is the quality of the environment there, in the everyday world, that should concern us.

## THE PARADOX OF LEISURE

It is sometimes argued that urban surroundings are relatively unimportant, since the metropolitan resident can always "get away from it all." The very job that requires him to live in an apartment or crowded subdivision also provides him with the income and leisure time to escape to more pleasant climes. Only if he is fortunate enough to live in certain older urban neighborhoods, however, is he likely to find respite near at hand: beautiful century-old Lincoln Park on Chicago's Near North Side is a noteworthy example of a facility established by citizens who regarded the city as a place to live in, not to escape from. But residents of other, newer areas all too often find such resources either non-existent or derelict owing to lack of civic concern.

Even when facilities within or near the metropolitan area are well-maintained, however, they are nearly always overcrowded. Ten thousand people descend on the Morton Arboretum on an autumn Sunday. Picnic tables in the Forest Preserves are practically unobtainable on a summer weekend. Golfers rise before dawn; boaters bribe for moorings.

The only alternative is to climb in the car and head for the country. Metropolitan residents join the mass exodus to distant beaches, campgrounds, private hideaways, or they simply engage in the favorite American pastime, "going for a drive."[3]

This leisure pattern, duplicated in every city by all the weekend vacationers who can afford it, is fast reaching a point of diminishing returns. As the rush to desirable rural spots grows with population and increase in disposable income, the very rurality of the destination declines. As the cities sprawl in all directions, yesterday's holiday community becomes today's commuter suburb: witness Hyde Park and the Chain-O-Lakes region. Longer journeys must be undertaken to reach ever more crowded retreats. Heavier traffic multiplies traveling time and frustration.

The paradox of leisure in contemporary America is that the cost in time, money, and frayed nerves threatens to exceed the obtainable physical and spiritual benefit. For the poor, the sick, and the aged, that point has already been reached: they stay at home. It will soon be reached for increasing numbers of their more affluent neighbors as their metropolitan habitat spreads in all directions. Part of the paradox is that even as leisure time and disposable income become more widely available, more people will decide more often to remain at home. "Man for the first time is destined to become almost totally metropolitan on a gargantuan scale. This means that he will live most of his days densely packed within a man-made environment."[4]

The paradox of leisure magnifies the importance of preserving environmental quality *within* the urban region. Man cannot live comfortably or healthfully in an uninterrupted continuum of impermeable surfaces, polluted resources, visual monotony, and cheek-by-jowl density. His elemental needs for earth, air, water, beauty, variety, and occasional solitude will encounter increasing frustration as the urban colossus becomes more oppressive. It is appalling to contemplate the living conditions for urban man if he neglects to conserve the natural resources of his metropolitan home, particularly those inherent to open land.

## THE OPEN LAND RESOURCE

As "country" beyond the metropolitan area recedes beyond practical distances, the importance of open spaces preserved *within* the urban region will vastly magnify. Long-neglected parks and recreation facilities will experience new demands as the family automobile ceases to be a feasible instrument of escape. Children of inner city and suburb alike will experience direct contact with nature only in "outdoor environmental centers." Established to preserve remnants of forest, prairie, moraine, bog, or dune, such centers would serve for the native landforms as the zoo does for the buffalo and the whooping crane.

The needs for preserved open land would not be limited to public recreation grounds and ecological study areas. According to a recent survey of the needs of the metropolitan areas for the next fifty years:

> Public open space does not now, and probably will never comprise more than a small share of the open space required in the metropolitan region. Some [open space] is required to provide visual breaks in an otherwise continuous and often dreary developed region. Some

of it will be required to make movement in the open space corridor more efficient, safer and pleasanter. . . . Some of it will be required for . . . thermal and hydrological effects.[5]

In other words, open space in private ownership, although providing no public access, is a highly valuable resource for the future metropolis. A proposed law to protect private open space expresses its importance as follows:

> The Legislature hereby finds that land in private ownership having a predominantly natural or agricultural character benefits the people of Illinois by refreshing the common air, by facilitating natural drainage and flood runoff, by replenishment of groundwater aquifers, by providing refuge to the native flora and fauna of Illinois, and by providing scenic enjoyment to users of public rights of way.[6]

The concept that preservation of open land in private hands serves the public interest is the foundation of the British system of Green Belts. The public authorities there, as here, could not afford to buy outright all the land required to keep "country" within reach of the city. Therefore they decided to restrain development on certain open areas surrounding London and other major cities. Private land owners continued to use their land as before and were compensated for the value taken by the restriction, upon denial of a permit to build on the land.

The metropolitan Green Belt idea has not been employed in this country. Partial belts of public holdings such as the Cook County Forest Preserves may serve to buffer urban areas from one another. But no major governmental effort has yet been made to preserve open land in *private* ownership.

On the contrary, the pressure upon property owners to yield to urbanization is itself the unfortunate, if unintended, result of governmental tax and housing policies. The great housing boom since World War II has been financed primarily through Federal Housing Administration and Veterans Administration loan guarantees. Both of these agencies have sponsored single family homes on the urban fringe in preference to any other form of new construction.

*Figure 2.   The geometry of Older Chicago. Residential áreas laid out between 1900 and 1930 follow rigid grid pattern, tempered by community park, school playgrounds, and well-shaded streets. Photo by the author.*

Federal tax law favors home ownership by allowing interest payments on home mortgages to be deducted from taxable income, whereas no such benefit is available to tenants. Finally, income used to pay rent is subject to income taxation whereas homeowners are not taxed on the "imputed rental" value of their homes. Taxwise, it pays to sprawl.

Private home ownership in amenable surroundings for the largest possible number of people is a highly appropriate national policy. But the commitment of every acre of metropolitan real estate to the realization of this dream will surely defeat its very purpose. The preservation of open land, whether in public or private hands, must be recognized as indispensable to "The American Dream."

## NORTHEASTERN ILLINOIS

It is perhaps prophetic that Chicago's street numbering system extends far out into the prairie of the west and south. No metropolitan area in America can match the Chicago Region in propensity to sprawl. Unimpeded by topographical barriers, the city has expanded continuously and symmetrically inland from its birthplace at the juncture of the Chicago River and Lake Michigan. The great mass of built-up area had a radius of 6 miles in 1900, 10 miles in 1930, and 15 miles in 1960. (The area subject to urban growth accordingly increases with the square of this radius.) (Figure 3.)

Extending like fingers from the central mass are the series of older suburbs strung out along commuter rail lines built during the early decades of the century.[7] Superimposed on the rail-line pattern is a new and farther-reaching system of limited-access expressways—the Kennedy, Eisenhower, Stevenson, Dan Ryan, and Skyway radial routes, and a primary circumferential road, the Illinois Tollway. As Figure 4 clearly illustrates, most new residential development follows the pattern of these expressways. The heaviest concentrations spring up where two or more of the new roads come close together. The recent opening of Interstate 80, combined with the efforts of Will County to attract industry, will doubtless stimulate a surge of development in the southern part of the metropolitan area.

Ten thousand acres of northeast Illinois farmland are being converted to residential use every year.[8] This pace is not likely to slow down, if forecasts for the region are even approximately on target. The present population of about 6.7 million will increase 50 percent to 9.3 million by 1990. The most

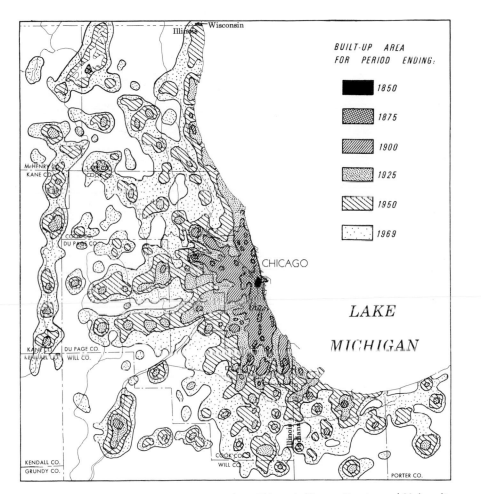

*Figure 3. Built-up areas for different periods in Chicago's history. Courtesy of University of Chicago, Center for Urban Studies.*

*Figure 4. The geometry of Megalopolis. Far out in the cornfields southwest of Chicago, new development arises next to the Stevenson Expressway. Compare with Figure 2 as to internal open space. No community park is provided in this brand new community. Photo by the author.*

significant feature of this estimate, however, is that virtually all of the growth will occur *outside the central cities*. The population of Chicago proper is expected to remain almost static at 3.5 to 4 million. Meanwhile, the six counties surrounding the city will jump from 2 million in 1960 to 6 million a generation later—an increase of 300 percent![9] Although population density will of course still be greatest near the central city, it is safe to predict that the pressure for residential development will reach every acre of northeastern Illinois. Unless action is taken now to set aside certain open spaces, the creeping tide of development will simply engulf the entire region.

## LAND WORTH SAVING: A PHYSICAL VIEW OF THE REGION

To appreciate the problems and opportunities for open lands, it is important to understand the natural characteristics of the region. Figure 5 shows that Chicago is the focal point of a series of concentric zones formed by vast ice sheets which buried the area and, as they melted, created Lake Chicago, the predecessor of Lake Michigan.

The innermost zone, the Lake Plain, was in fact the bed of the prehistoric lake, which was almost 60 feet higher than Lake Michigan today. The successive shorelines are marked by beach ridges visible in Chicago in the form of small hills, some of them quite steep, as along Longwood Drive in the southwestern part of the City. These ridges, well-drained and therefore wooded, are generally occupied by residences and cemeteries. The remainder of the Lake Plain itself is flat, poorly drained, unsuited to agriculture, and generally uninteresting in its natural state. Its use for urban development is not inappropriate, although careful over-all planning preservation of man-made parks should be vigorously encouraged.

Beyond the Lake Plain the landscape becomes suddenly more distinctive and arresting. Bordering Lake Michigan at either end of the plain are two of the most unusual formations in the Midwest, the bluff and ravine terrain of Chicago's settled northern suburbs and, of special interest, the famed Indiana Dunes along the southern shore. The expanse of "living dunes" created by a 300-mile "fetch" of wind and waves is equal to those in Oregon or Cape Cod. The dunes are constantly in motion, alternately burying and resurrecting whole forests, supporting a unique ecological system of the greatest

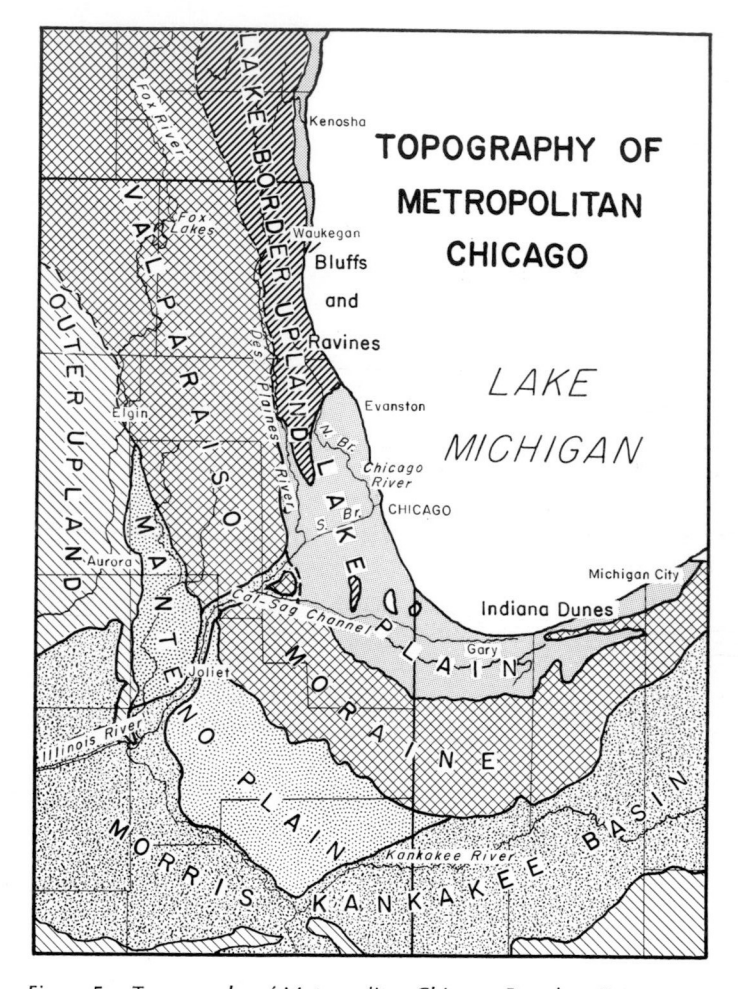

*Figure 5.    Topography of Metropolitan Chicago. Based on F. M. Fryxell,* The Physiography of the Region of Chicago.

interest to scientists and students. As a public recreation resource they offer contact with an everchanging and self-rejuvenating landscape.

Fatefully, the dunes are located midway between the Lake Superior iron deposits and the Illinois coalfields, with water access to both. In 1906 United States Steel began flattening duneland for its plants, and the process has continued to the present day. As recently as 1966 Bethlehem Steel leveled a 4,000-acre tract (selling the sand, incidentally, to Northwestern University for landfill). The adamant resistance of the Save the Dunes Council and other private conservation groups has not succeeded in halting the construction of immense plants, although it has salvaged remaining scraps of shoreline and some unspoiled inland territory for a National Lakeshore Park.[10]

The fate of the North Shore Bluffs for residential occupancy and the Indiana Dunes for industrial and residential use has been irrevocably decided. Little shoreline remains for public use, although the voters of Highland Park have very recently approved a 15-million-dollar bond issue to purchase the site of the Moraine-on-the-Lake Hotel, thus sparing a prime specimen of bluff terrain from high-rise apartment development. Only in Chicago itself, thanks to the foresight of Daniel Burnham in 1909, is the shoreline devoted chiefly to public parks. In even shorter supply than recreational areas are open spaces where the bluffs and dunes remain undisturbed in their natural state.

If the development of the shore areas is an accomplished fact, the time for decision is still at hand for a much larger if less dramatic inland landscape. Surrounding the Lake Plain like the rim of a bowl is a broad crescent of higher ground known as the Valparaiso Upland. Formed by the piling up of debris at the leading edge of glacial ice, this terminal moraine varies in width from 12 to 25 miles. Its inner edge is followed approximately by the Illinois Tollway, and it lies partly in each of the six northeastern Illinois counties.

The characteristically uneven upland moraine is poorly suited to agriculture but is well drained and marked by numerous lakes and bogs. The rough topography is especially distinctive in the "knob and kettle" terrain of Lake and McHenry counties. The hills and depressions are less prominent further south in DuPage, Cook, and Will, but sloughs, bogs, and groves dot these counties.[11]

Broad expressways tend to obscure the sharp transition from plain to upland, but the change is inescapable for travellers on any east-west street. Fifty-fifth Street, for instance, which bisects the

Lake Plain at its widest point, moves across flat industrialized land to the Tollway and the Cook County boundary. But, approaching Hinsdale in DuPage County, the road begins to weave and swoop through steep little hills. Majestic old oaks and sycamores canopy the streets. One has entered the moraine, a scenic natural boundary 6 miles beyond the Chicago city limits.

Although pastures and cornfields are common between settled areas in the upland, the rolling hills and thin topsoil are far from ideal for farming. But the well-drained, gravelly limestone base is unusually suitable for trees, as the Morton Arboretum has dramatically demonstrated by successfully introducing 5,000 varieties of woody plants in moraine soil.

The woods, drainage, and varied relief typical of the moraine render it highly attractive to residential developers. The amenities of tree cover and wooded surroundings is reflected in the sylvan names of older communities: Elk Grove, Downers Grove, Buffalo Grove, Homewood, and the plethora of towns beginning with "Oak." (Many less-than-candid entrepreneurs today give names like "Evergreen Park" even to new developments on the treeless plain.) Pressure to turn the desirable upland into one vast bedroom belt mounts with every passing day and year.

New transportation patterns increase the vulnerability of the entire moraine to exclusively residential development. The finger pattern of suburban growth along commuter railroad lines once tended to protect "green wedges" of land in between. But now the radial expressways, most of them routed through these interstitial wedges in order to save land acquisition costs and avoid disruption of established communities, put every property in the six counties within commuting range of the Loop or one of the outlying centers of employment. As land values rise, no land owner will be sheltered from rising taxes or from seductive offers by developers to relieve him of that burden.

The Northeastern Illinois Planning Commission report entitled "Diversity Within Order" urges retention of the finger pattern with open areas between:

> Open space land should be reserved between the fingers as close as possible to the Chicago Loop. Particular attention should be given to maximizing natural resource utilization and reducing hazards to urban development.[12]

Because commuting patterns are no longer oriented to rail facilities, however, this recommendation is not likely to be heeded. It will take the concerted effort of aroused citizens and conscientious land owners to prevent the closing in of spaces between—and beyond—the fingers.

The Valparaiso Upland is by no means an unlimited resource. One geographer has estimated that the Illinois portion amounts to about 900 square miles, tapering in width from about 25 miles near the Wisconsin border to about 10 miles at the Indiana line.[13] Should development succeed in burying the moraine, there would be no natural barrier to the urban tide. The excellent farmland of the Outer Upland and the Manteno Plain around the border of the crescent would fan out to a radius of 60 miles before being arrested at the Kankakee Valley. Portents of the future can already be detected in the push northward toward Milwaukee and westward toward DeKalb and Rockford. (See Appendix III.)

The prospect of sprawl on such a gigantic scale should be of concern not only to the owner of open lands but to all of his neighbors. The promise of instant fortune that tempts the property holder must be balanced against the certainty that the beauty of his land and its natural benefits to future generations will be obliterated by construction. Even if the owner is unperturbed by such misgivings, those who gain simply from his land's openness—the homeowner next to a woodlot, the bird-watcher near a swamp, the downstream inhabitants of a floodplain, indeed everyone who cares for natural beauty—have a right and a responsibility to seek a better answer.

There *are* better answers, for both the concerned landowner and the concerned citizen. Some of them are illustrated in the following chapter through case histories of individuals and groups who have acted as "open land advocates" in the Chicago region. Alternatives open to the property owner are spelled out in succeeding chapters, where the techniques of responsible "land stewardship" are described in detail. Neither the owner nor his neighbor need feel helpless before the threat of sprawl. Prompt and vigilant action can still rescue "space where nobody is" for everybody to enjoy.

*Figure 6. Peacock Prairie, a 5-acre remnant of unplowed Illinois black soil prairie, is located near the town of Glenview in Cook County. The "rattlesnake master" is among hundreds of distinctive species which it contains. Photo by Forrest Emerson.*

## 2
## OPEN LAND ADVOCACY—THE CITIZEN'S ROLE

### WHO IS A LAND ADVOCATE?

This chapter introduces the unsung hero (or more frequently, heroine) of land preservation —the citizen "open land advocate." Armed with petitions, maps, photographs, and philosophy, the enlightened amateur can profoundly affect the seemingly inexorable course toward development. Planners' dogmas, attorneys' maxims, and the city fathers' economics all may wither before the arguments of the aroused and informed private citizen.

The land advocate bears little resemblance to the traditional "dear lady in tennis shoes," except that some do happen to be dear ladies who wear tennis shoes. While the legendary version was a caricature of kindly ineffectuality, today's land advocate cannot so easily be put off. All the techniques of political action up to and including lawsuits and constitutional amendments are within the competence of the astute amateur conservationist today.

The land advocate may also be distinguished from the hand-wringer or fist-shaker. When development threatens to ravage a favorite beauty spot or natural curiosity, many would-be protectors indulge in futile rhetoric or invective. Unreasonable demands beget stubborn refusals, and the land is lost.

The land advocate recognizes that the conflict is one of mutually inconsistent vested interests. He and his neighbors benefit from the openness of nearby land which they don't own. The owner, however, often is chiefly interested in maximizing the economic yield of such land. In rural areas, the best economic return is from agriculture, so the land remains open (although not in a wild condition). If metropolitan land values reach the site as the city spreads outward, the best return is derived from urban development. At that point the interests of the owner and his neighbors become incompatible.

If the land is developed, the owner benefits and the neighbors suffer a cost in terms of harm to their environment. If the land is not permitted to be developed, the neighbors retain a benefit at the cost to the owner of lost income. It is the difficulty of allocating to the benefited party the cost of providing such a benefit that makes open land disputes both complicated and emotional.

Development is not inherently bad. The President's Commission on Urban Housing calls for 26 million homes to be built in the next ten years to replace our aging stock. Industrial and commercial development provide jobs and indirectly support the local school budget through their tax payments. Even highways, the scourge of most conservationists, facilitate both economic and recreational mobility.

But while development frequently serves the public need for homes and jobs, non-development sometimes serves other, deeper needs of the spirit. Man-made facilities can be placed almost anywhere; unusual natural phenomena must be enjoyed where found. The former are transient; the latter enduring, if left alone. To obliterate a unique natural area for the sake of an artificial thing therefore is utterly senseless.

The land advocate is a citizen who recognizes this senselessness and takes action to prevent it. Rallying others to the cause, the land advocate is the prime mover in any conservation effort.

## LEGAL RESOURCES OF LAND ADVOCACY

The first resort of the land advocate, of course, is to appeal to the owner's sense of civic responsibility by pointing out the opportunities for land stewardship (to be described in the next chapter). In such cases, an attorney probably will be needed to present the proposal since laymen cannot give legal advice. Anyone familiar with the concepts of land stewardship, however, may promote them in a non-technical fashion. Depending upon the circumstances of the land and the owner, the land advocate may succeed in procuring a donation of part or all of the property.

Failing an appeal for voluntary dedication or donation, the next resort in most landsaving situations is to determine whether a proposed change in land use may be prevented through the zoning power or other application of the public authority to regulate land. Non-compensatory regulations, however, are subject to stringent constitutional safeguards against "unreasonable" deprivation of the owner's right to use his land.

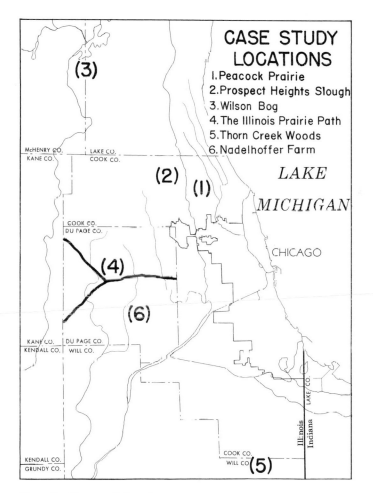

Figure 7. Case study locations.

An exercise of the zoning power must be reasonably related to the protection of the public health, safety, or welfare. A total ban on development of private land would be considered "unreasonable," unless the land happened to be located in a flood plain, a peat bog, on a mud slope, or other hazardous situation.

A developer of land may be required under public regulatory powers to provide open space only to the extent of the need generated by development of the balance of the property. Thus a single house may be subject to set-back and minimum lot size requirements. A subdivision developer may be required to provide open space commensurate with the needs of his project, but not in satisfaction of the needs of the public-at-large.

Aside from these constitutional restraints on non-compensatory regulations of land use, this avenue of land advocacy may be impeded by political considerations. The local public body which exercises jurisdiction over the land is likely to be the owner/developer's natural ally. Development, particularly of a non-residential nature, improves the local tax base, and many city fathers believe construction is synonymous with progress. Thus the land advocate who testifies against a zoning change to permit such development may be in a weak position indeed.

Having exhausted land stewardship arguments and regulatory possibilities, the land advocate's final resort is to attempt to procure sufficient private or public funds to purchase the property. If the owner is willing to sell for a reasonable price, the task is simply that of finding the money. If he is unwilling, some public agency having the power of condemnation, as well as money, must act swiftly enough to prevent the loss of the qualities which are to be saved.

As the following case studies indicate, the problems of raising private and/or public money are substantial. Only in rare cases can the people who will be most benefited by open space be exactly identified and persuaded to purchase it. A major public campaign is often required, entailing a formal organization, adequate press coverage, and sustained effort over a period of years.

The case studies below are all taken from the records of the Open Lands Project. They concern five different kinds of open space facilities scattered through metropolitan Chicago: prairie, footpath, slough, bog, and woods. Each area is essentially of local interest, although in some cases their scientific reputation is much wider. These are portraits of open land advocacy in action.

## 1. Peacock Prairie

There are some residents of Glenview who feel that Peacock Prairie could well be renamed Popelka Prairie, for it was Bernice Popelka's nearly three-year battle against formidable obstacles that saved the tiny tract of virgin land.

Peacock Prairie is a 5-acre remnant of original black soil Illinois prairie. Held by the Long family from the day of the original federal grant in 1842, it was acquired from the Longs by the Peacock family in the 1930s. Somehow the little scrap of land escaped the plow and intensive grazing, continuing intact even as the area around it changed from prairie to farm to shopping center. More than a hundred varieties of true prairie plants thrust their roots deep into the black earth, forming a closed system that wards off the intrusion of alien weeds.

Mrs. Popelka, introduced to the prairie tract by a friend one day in 1965, was enthralled by the miniature museum of a lost landscape. A housewife well versed in botany and experienced in political action, she determined that it must be saved. A speech on the vanishing landscape by Professor Hugh Iltis of the University of Wisconsin helped to strengthen her resolve.

The location of the prairie made the cause of preservation seem hopeless. The land is marooned between two major highways, difficult to reach on foot but ideally situated for a high-rise office building. As the Illinois Director of Conservation later commented, it would be "practically impossible to preserve it as a prairie because of its location and the urban encroachment which will undoubtedly continue."

Yet Mrs. Popelka soon found allies. Naturalists of the Chicago area offered advice and support. Many were familiar with the prairie and had brought classes there for field study. She also received the backing of local conservation organizations, including the Open Lands Project. In November of 1965, she and a small cadre of Glenview residents formed the Peacock Prairie Preservation Committee.

The chief problem the group had to face was the sheer economic worth of the land. Its strategic location made it too valuable to rescue through noncompensatory measures or a temporary lease arrangement. The owner, Arthur T. McIntosh, was a Chicago realtor fully aware of the potential for development. While not unsympathetic to the committee's purpose, he replied when approached that November: "I can't afford to be a philanthropist. I'm not opposed to renting the property but I must be realistic."[14]

It was obvious that the only course open was outright purchase. The question was, who would help?

The group appealed first to the Cook County Forest Preserve District. But their request was turned down because the superintendent, Charles "Cap" Sauers, felt that the plot was too small and too expensive. Since Sauers was also chairman of the Illinois Conservation Advisory Board, his view later prevailed at the state level as well.

The main recourse open to the prairie advocates was to enlist the support of the Glenview Park District. If it would accept donations amounting to half the purchase price, the District could then apply for the other half from the federal open space program. Lacking proof that the private half could actually be raised, however, the district decided to table the proposal indefinitely.

In February 1966 the Peacock committee became incorporated and began a fund-raising campaign. Through public speeches and newspaper publicity they invited citizens to write in support of their effort and to send contributions. The Chicago dailies and North Shore suburban papers carried well-illustrated stories on the prairie.

Meanwhile the prairie itself was under immediate threat, emerging from winter in sorry state. Its advocates were appalled to discover in late March that tons of trash, previously hidden by vegetation and snow, were littering much of the ground. Mrs. Popelka promptly organized local children to help her clear away the junk. Four large loads were removed with the aid of a donated truck. Mrs. Popelka rented another truck and drove out with the fifth load herself. With the coming of spring the prairie recovered its resplendent garb.

Another threat materialized that summer. The land was under lease to an outdoor amusements concession. In July the lessee began mowing down the prairie growth to clear space for an archery range and a baseball batting game. The instant it was discovered, Bernice Popelka went directly to the home of Jeffrey Short, President of the Open Lands Project, for emergency counsel. Mr. Short sent a wire to Arthur McIntosh, who in turn prevailed on the amusements firm to cease mowing. Shortly thereafter, McIntosh expressed interest in inspecting his property first hand and received a tour escorted by some of the area's prominent botanists. Evidently impressed, he persuaded the lessee to refrain from disturbing the prairie further, but he remained noncommittal about how long he would continue to sustain the resulting loss of rental revenue.

Late in 1966 the University of Illinois Circle Campus consented to accept the property as a gift and use it as a botanical research center. The trustees authorized an appraisal by the Real Estate Research Corporation, which set a value of $210,000 on the 5.14 acres. Having found an eminently suitable recipient for the prairie, the only problem for its advocates was to raise the money.

Publicity had generated wide interest but a far from encouraging sum in donations. During 1967 the fund-raising burden shifted from the Peacock committee to the Open Lands Project. Mrs. Popelka and her group tirelessly continued the indispensable effort to stimulate and maintain public support. A highlight of their work was the exhibit of prairie plants at the Chicago Flower Show in the spring.

Board members of the Open Lands Project, and especially its executive director, Gunnar A. Peterson, approached many individuals and philanthropic organizations for the private half of the purchase price. Since the university was a qualified applicant, parallel requests for 50 percent funding were also filed with the Department of Housing and Urban Development (HUD) and the Bureau of Outdoor Recreation (BOR). Both Illinois senators and numerous other public figures actively endorsed the applications.

After an unremitting campaign by the Open Lands Project, the Chicago Community Trust agreed in April 1967 to donate the entire private share. But the application to HUD was denied, and the BOR request was delayed pending a revision of the Illinois Recreation Plan and a thaw in the federal freeze on expenditures. BOR also expressed dismay about the lack of "recreational potential" offered by the prairie.

The federal logjam was finally broken in December 1967, and BOR "unofficially" promised its share. Negotiations with the owner and lessee were successfully completed on the basis of the established appraisal value. In May 1968 the University of Illinois took title to Peacock Prairie. Fencing and the construction of an interpretation center are currently being completed under a donation received from Mr. John Leslie.

The story of Peacock Prairie provides a classic example of the vigorous effort which land advocacy can and must expend to overcome the logic of land economics. It took two and a half years and appeals to every level of government as well as to private sources, but the prairie has been preserved for the delight and edification of future generations. Although she has since moved to Wisconsin, Bernice Popelka still keeps a vigilant eye on Peacock Prairie.

## 2. Prospect Heights Slough

A slough does not sound like a beautiful place. According to Webster, it is "a place of deep mud or mire; a creek in a marsh." Its associated psychological meaning is "a state of moral degradation or spiritual dejection."

Webster notwithstanding, the residents of Prospect Heights in Cook County feel quite the opposite about their slough. In the words of Mrs. Fred Hedemark, the wild area at the foot of her driveway is a "God-made beauty spot, a lovely lagoon, with ducks, raccoons, rabbits, pheasants, fish and perhaps other wildlife."

The slough in Prospect Heights lies in a depression between two moraine ridges. It consists of a pond surrounded by a narrow belt of wetland thickly covered with low-lying shrubbery and cat-tails affording refuge to wildlife. Thus the slough is a micro-sanctuary for animals and birds displaced by urbanization of the surrounding landscape.

Unlike a bog, a slough forms part of an active drainage system. The Prospect Heights slough is a link in the MacDonald Creek tributary system which eventually drains into the Des Plaines River. As the surrounding land is increasingly paved or built over, run-off from storms becomes an increasingly serious problem. The Prospect Heights slough is an important natural "sponge," capturing storm run-off in its lagoon rather than allowing it to flood low-lying areas downstream. Even with the slough, a 1967 flood caused $42,000 in property damage along MacDonald Creek.

22

*Figure 8. Prospect Heights Slough, a 13-acre wetland in the midst of northwest Cook County sprawl. It serves as a natural floodwater retention pond and provides refuge to birds and other wildlife. Photo by the author.*

The original developer of Prospect Heights thirty years ago left the slough alone, recognizing that it would be unwise if not impossible to build in a natural drainage area. Besides, the lagoon was known to be underlain with peat, making the cost of filling prohibitive. The developer was content to build his homes along the ridges overlooking the slough, leaving the wet area for the aesthetic, recreational, and hydrologic benefit of the local residents.

Unfortunately, this ecological relationship was not given legal recognition. The residents of the subdivision simply enjoyed the presence of the slough without formal divestment of the owner's title being made. (By contrast, the home owners bordering a downstream portion of the lagoon formed an association to purchase and hold title to their share of the wetland.)

The developer retired to Florida and failed to pay taxes on his slough. In 1968 it was sold by Cook County for back taxes to a Chicago builder. Land values in the area had so vastly appreciated that it now appeared economically feasible to undertake the expense of filling the lagoon.

Mrs. Fred Hedemark is a housewife with no formal training in ecology, but she clearly perceived the value of the slough as a natural area worth saving. Although she and her husband plan to retire and leave the community soon, she saw no reason to permit the slough to be lost by default.

Spying a heavy dump truck unloading into the slough one morning, Mrs. Hedemark hailed the driver and demanded to see his dumping permit. He produced one signed by the Township Commissioner of Roads. The Hedemarks telephoned the commissioner, who denied any knowledge of the dumping and agreed with their contention that it was illegal to operate a 10-ton truck on a road limited to 5 tons. He revoked the permit.

The owner of the slough then resorted to legal procedure, filing application with the Cook County Board of Zoning Appeals for a special use permit to fill the slough. Since the area was unincorporated, county zoning was applicable.

Cook County zoning procedure requires notice of a proposed change to be posted on the land itself as well as in newspapers. In April 1969 the notice of a hearing to be held three weeks later appeared on telephone poles near the slough. Mrs. Hedemark and a band of neighbors went to the hearing in the nearby Village of Wheeling. The room was filled with protesters, but the owner failed to show up, pleading illness of his attorney. The hearing was postponed until June. Again the residents appeared but the applicant did not, this time because he reported he was replacing his attorney.

Before the next rescheduled hearing, Mrs Hedemark wrote to the Open Lands Project for assistance. On the basis of her information and our own research, we prepared a petition entitled "Proxy Objection." Following a legal description of the property, the form read:

> The highest and best use of the property in question is in the form of natural open space. As a water collection lagoon, its existence is vital to the prevention of flooding of surrounding land. As a haven for indigenous plants, birds, and other wildlife, its preservation is essential to the character of this rapidly urbanizing section of Cook County. The destruction of this lagoon through filling in and construction would deprive the County of one of its last remaining wildlife sanctuaries and would endanger human life and property through flooding.
>
> The undersigned therefore object(s) to the granting of any permit to the petitioner which would have the result of filling in, or changing the natural condition of the property in question.

The recommendation that the zoning power be used to prevent development was based on the danger of flooding which filling of the slough would create.

During the next few weeks Mrs. Hedemark and her neighbors diligently circulated this petition, explaining that it would place a signer's objection before the Zoning Board if he could not personally attend. Copies were signed by 161 residents of the surrounding area. One was received from the members of the volunteer fire department, which mentioned the need to draw water from the slough in the event of fire. Another was signed by members of the local post office.

Residents attending the final scheduled hearing were joined by representatives of the Prospect Heights Park District. A local attorney was also present, to represent the neighborhood and to offer the proxy objections. Once again the owner pleaded for a continuance on the grounds of illness. The Board denied the motion and dismissed the application.

This anticlimactic "victory" only ensured that the slough would be preserved until the owner should file a new application or undertake illegal dumping. It was apparent that the slough must be purchased by the Park District, by a home owners association, or by a philanthropic individual in order to protect it permanently. Mrs. Hedemark as land advocate for the neighborhood continued to work on the problem. Just recently the slough was listed in the comprehensive plan of the Prospect Heights Park District for future acquisition as a wetlands park.

### 3. Wilson Bog

At its northwest extremity the Chicago metropolitan area laps into McHenry County, which was until the past decade a scenic mosaic of villages, estates, and farms far removed from urbanism and its attendant problems. Only in the vicinity of the Chain O'Lakes was there concentrated residential development, chiefly summer cottages.

With the outward thrust of the Chicago area population, however, the landscape of eastern McHenry County took on the signs of helter-skelter conversion to urban uses so characteristic of land-boom communities closer to the Loop. The Chain O'Lakes homes were adapted for year-round use; new commuter subdivisions sprang up around lesser lakes and ponds. The Village of McHenry's population doubled between 1950 and 1965 from 50,000 to 100,000. Three-fold increases occurred in the eastern townships of Nunda, Algonquin, and McHenry.

Despite the extensive new home construction underway in the eastern part of the county, however, a considerable semblance of rurality persists. Thanks to the glacial "plow" which heaped the landscape into hills and depressions ("knobs and kettles"), one is not so constantly within view of development as on the flatter Lake Plain. New communities have typically been clustered around the many small lakes or ponds in an effort to achieve a "vacation" atmosphere. The interlaken uplands remain to a large extent in farms or woods. These factors help perpetuate the illusion that McHenry remains undisturbed. This illusion has caused the defeat of two referenda to create a county forest preserve district: "Why should I pay for public open space if I am surrounded by private open land as far as my eye can see?"

*Figure 9. The Volo Tamarack Bog in western Lake County was the subject of much public attention when a developer proposed to build a golf course on its border. The Volo Bog, which is an Illinois Nature Preserve, is about 2 miles from the Wilson Bog.*

But private land is no longer quite so open. McHenry's beautiful hills are packed with sand and gravel piled up by the glacier. Owners of land no longer profitable to farm but not yet ripe for development frequently resort to leasing gravel rights. Many a once magnificent view is now marred by the gashes of gravel pits and processing facilities; the right to exploit private land is thus carried to its ugliest extreme.

It was with the greatest dismay that residents of the Worthmore and Bay View subdivisions near Pistakee Lake on the McHenry-Lake County line learned of plans for a 55-acre gravel pit to be dug across the road from their homes. The prospect of a scarred landscape, dust, noise, and gargantuan trucks on their road aroused them to opposition.

Mining of gravel is not restricted by zoning in McHenry County, but the supporting activities of washing, sorting, crushing, etc., require a conditional use permit to be issued by the County Board of Zoning Appeals. It was against the granting of this permit that the neighborhood's opposition was directed.

While the residents' revolt was concerned primarily with the preservation of property values in the subdivisions to the north of the proposed site, the leaders of a "Concerned Citizens Group" took a broader view of the problem. They perceived that the ill effects of the mining operation would not only spill over to the *residential* community, but also to an *ecological* community which borders the site on the east. This community is known to old-timers of the area as well as to botanists of the Midwest as the Wilson Bog, the largest of several tamarack bogs in the McHenry-Lake County area.

Tamarack bogs are characteristic of glacial country. Found in great numbers in northern Michigan, Minnesota, and Wisconsin, they are rare in Illinois. As the ice receded some ten thousand years ago, giant blocks left in the ground gradually melted and became ponds or lakes. Over thousands of years, some of these bodies of water which lacked any natural drainage outlets acquired a heavy mat of vegetation, primarily sphagnum moss. The mat thickened until it could support forests of tamarack on a surface so shaky that a child can make trees quake by jumping up and down.

Owing to its hydrologic isolation, a bog is an ecosystem divorced from the outside world. More acidic than surrounding uplands, it maintains a plant community peculiar to the Age of

Reptiles, including orchids and carnivorous pitcher plants. The accumulation of peat under the sphagnum surface holds relics of ancient climates and life forms, which can be tapped through core samples and pollen analysis. In short, the tamarack bog is a museum not merely of past centuries, as with Peacock Prairie, but of past millennia.

Coincidentally, another bog, located a mile southeast of Wilson in Lake County, was much in the news at the time the "Concerned Citizens Group" was planning its campaign: The *Chicago Tribune* ran a series on the Volo Bog in June 1970. It had been bought by the Nature Conservancy for the University of Illinois to use as an ecological laboratory. A developer was applying for zoning permission to build a golf course up to the Bog's edge. Opposition to this prospect from Chicago area conservationists redounded to the benefit of the Wilson Bog group. The newspapers and the public generally were much excited about the necessity of saving such natural phenomena, despite the physical difficulty of getting into a bog.

It was not clear to what extent the Wilson Bog would be affected by a gravel pit 1,000 feet away. In search of more expert opinion, Mrs. Lori Huml, a leader of the group, consulted the *National Geographic*, the Open Lands Project, the Illinois Geologic Survey in Naperville, the Natural Resource Service Center at the Morton Arboretum, and various Chicago area natural scientists. No one could give positive predictions, except to say that *any* impact would be deterimental. The viability of a bog depends upon its insulation from the world around it. Since the bog lay downwind from the gravel site and since water flows from the upland into depressions, it appeared likely that harmful impact in one form or another would occur.

What appeared at the outset as a routine case of community opposition to a local nuisance was thus translated into a major conservation battle. The conflict shared in the regional publicity accorded the Volo Bog, culminating in an NBC-TV "special" on the two bogs which Mrs. Huml helped to arrange.

The first zoning hearing on the gravel application in August 1969 was a haphazard affair. Sixty local residents unrepresented by counsel barraged the pit's proponents with enough questions to obtain a month's extension of the hearing.

29

At the next meeting, the objectors were represented by an attorney, whose retainer was paid through contributions. Lively cross-examination of the applicants' expert witness raised more concern about the Bog. The hearing was again extended, this time until October 15.

In preparation for a showdown, the citizens group acquired 479 signatures on a petition objecting to the permit. Fifty residents attended the hearing. A film of Wilson Bog was displayed to the Board, and expert testimony on the value of the area was presented by Elizabeth Lunn, professor of biology at Lake Forest College. An *amicus curiae* brief filed by the Open Lands Project provided additional information, concluding:

> It would be an irreparable loss to the citizens of the County and of the State if this area of wild, natural beauty were to be in the slightest way damaged by commercial enterprise.

Despite the excellent preparation for the hearing on the part of William Franz, attorney for the citizens group, one vital link in the legal machinery was missing. Unlike Volo Bog, which is publicly held, Wilson Bog is still owned privately—in part by the same party who owns the proposed gravel site. In the absence of objection from the Bog's actual owners, the Zoning Board granted the permit.

The next recourse for the opposition was the Board of Supervisors, the legislative arm of McHenry County. It is a function of that Board to review the decisions of the Board of Zoning Appeals. Ordinarily, a simple majority of the supervisors is sufficient to approve a zoning change. However, according to state law and county ordinance (which must follow the state law), a three-quarters majority is required to change zoning if timely written protest is made by:

> . . . the owners of twenty percent of the frontage proposed to be altered, or by the owners of twenty percent of the frontage immediately adjoining or across an alley therefrom, or by the owners of twenty percent of the frontage directly opposite the frontage proposed to be altered.—(Ill. Rev. Stat., Ch. 34, Sec. 3158)

Interpretation of this procedural gibberish proved to be vital to the case. In voting 15–9 (2 pass, 1 absent) in favor of the zoning change, the Board had failed to reach a three-quarters majority of its members. Confronted with 479 individual objections, including owners of more than 20 percent of the *perimeter* of the property proposed to be altered, the Board Chairman declared that approval was denied. The Bog's defenders were exultant.

Four months later, in April 1970, the applicants for the gravel permit filed suit in Circuit Court for a writ of mandamus against certain county officials to require them to grant the permit. The theory of the suit was that objections did not satisfy the legal requirements necessitating a three-quarters majority. In particular, the applicants argued that an owner of abutting property (not separated by a public thoroughfare) did not count under the "20 percent of frontage" rule.

The conservationists replied that the meaning of "frontage" was not clearly interpreted under Illinois law but that custom and common sense suggested that it should include owners around the perimeter of the property proposed to be rezoned. Otherwise, reasoned the objectors, a next-door neighbor lacking road frontage would not be included in the "20 percent classification" if he only had a fence between himself and the property proposed to be rezoned; if he were to dedicate a public alley along the fence line, however, he would then be counted!

Notwithstanding such anomalous possibilities, the court turned down the objectors' argument and decided in favor of the gravel pit. Although the decision rested on a dubious point of law, the Wilson Bog Committee decided not to appeal. They had raised over $2,000 through a lottery to pay their legal expenses to date and could see no hope of financing further litigation.

The thrust of the conservation efforts turned instead from a delaying action in the courts to an all-out campaign to obtain acquisition of the Bog by the State Department of Conservation. Mrs. Huml subscribed to "unlimited call-pak" telephone service so as to maintain hourly contact with officials in Springfield, Chicago, and Rockford. The key agencies capable of taking action were the Department of Conservation and the Nature Preserves Commission which serves as purchasing agent for the Department in northeastern Illinois. Mrs. Huml obtained strong backing from Joseph Karaganis, assistant attorney-general, and from the Chicago press and the Open Lands Project.

On the basis of the recommendations of George Fell of the Nature Preserves Commission, the Department of Conservation decided to undertake major acquisitions in the McHenry-Lake County glacial wetlands. The much publicized Volo Bog would be protected by the purchase of a 155-acre buffer zone from a development concern. Wilson Bog would be acquired together with a narrow upland buffer zone. Finally, as a complete surprise to conservationists, some 1,500 acres surrounding an unpolluted pond named Defiance Lake 3 miles southwest of Wilson Bog was also proposed for acquisition.

Still unresolved at this writing is whether the Wilson Bog Committee's original objective will be achieved, namely the prevention of a 55-acre gravel pit within a few hundred yards of the Bog. The buffer proposed by the Nature Preserves Commission would take only 6 acres from the proposed gravel site. The fear remains, therefore, that the pit will be operated and will damage the Bog itself through windborne dust and possible fluctuation of the ground water regime. With conflicting scientific opinion on the matter, however, the State disputes that its investment will be imperilled. It has apparently decided to err on the side of economy.

### 4. The Illinois Prairie Path

In 1903, the Chicago, Aurora, & Elgin Railroad inaugurated its electric commuter service between the Fox River Valley and the Chicago Loop. Its tracks ran through the western suburban "finger" containing Elmhurst, Villa Park, Lombard, Glen Ellyn, and Wheaton. West of Wheaton, the line split into branches serving Elgin, Geneva, Batavia, and Aurora. Part of the Insull complex, the C. A. & E. gave superb service for fifty years to both local householders and commuters.

As a limited-function interurban line, the C. A. & E. found competition difficult with major trunk lines such as the Chicago & Northwestern, whose route it paralleled in part. In later years, a dispute with the Chicago Transit Authority blocked the C. A. & E. from entering the elevated "loop," thus eliminating the electric line's main advantage. Construction of the Eisenhower Expressway siphoned off many of the remaining riders. Finally, in the late 1950s, the C. A. & E. abandoned all service, including freight. Its termination left a swath of unused land extending through the most heavily built-up areas in the west suburbs.

Neither Nature nor Man can tolerate a vacuum. Alternative proposals were heard—to use the strip for a highway, for sewers, for additional utility lines, for extensions of adjacent private property.

*Figure 10.   A land advocate in her element, Mrs. May Watts of the Morton Arboretum inspired the establishment of the Illinois Prairie Path.*

*Figure 11.* *The Prairie Path slices through built-up suburbs west of Wheaton on the former right-of-way of the Chicago, Aurora & Elgin interurban railroad. Photo by the author.*

Before any single recommendation could be crystallized into reality, however, an open land advocate made herself heard.

Mrs. May Theilgaard Watts is the retired Naturalist of the Morton Arboretum, famous for her writing, lectures, and classes dealing with the natural environment. Her book *Reading the Landscape* is used in many university courses in ecology. In all facets of her career, she has tried to promote awareness of the natural world as an experience to be enjoyed intimately and at first hand. She might be termed a "participatory naturalist."

Perhaps the record will one day show that Mrs. Watts's most influential piece of writing was her letter to the *Chicago Tribune* of September 25, 1963; in it she praised the English tradition of public footpaths and pointed out the opportunity to create a pathway on the disused C. A. & E. right-of-way.

The response was instantaneous. Mrs. Watts had evidently touched upon a basic concern of many people, namely, the loss of contact with natural phenomena in daily life. Residents of DuPage County communities through which the route would pass flocked to the cause. A leadership group arose, which was incorporated "not for profit" in 1964 as "The Illinois Prairie Path" (IPP). Its leading members over the next five years included residents of Naperville, Wayne, St. Charles, Geneva, Elmhurst, and Morton Grove.

These land advocates immediately set about the initial tasks of determining the ownership of the route and of publicizing their plan. Title to the various sections of the right-of-way proved to be a Gordian knot of stale claims, easements, outstanding tax bills, and reversionary interests. Some of the complex problems had already been explored by attorneys for DuPage County, whose supervisors recognized the route's potential "for future public multiple use." Since the IPP lacked the money for land and/or legal fees, as well as the power of eminent domain, the obvious necessity was to encourage the County supervisors to purchase the right-of-way and then to grant the IPP a lease for its surface use.

Most persuasive among the IPP methods of arousing voter interest was a ten-minute film strip, made with the help of the Open Lands Project and a film company, with projectors donated by a manufacturer. Shown to hundreds of residents and officials in the various contiguous communities, it aroused wide public sentiment for the project.

Vitally important to the establishment of the Path was a grant by Commonwealth Edison of permission to walk along its rights-of-way where they coincided with the C. A. & E. right-of-way. Also crucial was the assistance given by local residents in solving such specifically local problems as zoning or condemnation suits. Countless hours of volunteer help were devoted to publicizing the Path through radio, TV, lectures, and correspondence.

The major portion of the route was purchased by DuPage County for $400,000 from the railroad company. Both Commonwealth Edison and Northern Illinois Gas Company cooperated in conveying their interests to the County, subject to easements for their existng lines.

In May 1966 The Illinois Prairie Path group was granted its hard-earned twelve-year lease, since the footpath could be established compatibly with other public uses such as underground or overhead utility lines, and parking where necessary. Two municipalities did require parking spaces, but the continuity of the path was guaranteed: each municipality leasing the right-of-way within their borders from DuPage County was required to reserve a minimum 10-foot strip for the Prairie Path. (Sometimes it is hard indeed for the hiker to locate that strip, but the "right" is there, even if only between rows of parked cars).

Gradually the Path began to enjoy prestige in the form of support by public officials from the village level up to the rank of Cabinet member and Senator. On one of the first of its Annual Walks (October 1965), several hundred persons participated in 23 specialty field trips. The Prairie Path was cited nationally as an example of what enlightened citizen action could accomplish.

Membership dues provided IPP with working capital for mailing materials, for IPP signs, and for the necessary "general public liability insurance" policy. A formal agreement was reached with the Commonwealth Edison Company, and tax-deductible status for the Path as an educational "charitable institution" was finally achieved. A few restrictions were laid down: no motorized vehicles (except county and utility), no guns, no alcoholic beverages sold or used and, because of high tension wires, no flying of kites or model planes.

During the subsequent three years, 90 percent of the Path right-of-way was "adopted" by a wide variety of groups and individuals, in segments of varying size. These volunteer custodians, including Scouts, civic associations, garden clubs, Audubon societies, work in cooperation with IPP to plant, clean up trash, and develop rest areas or other special features.

The footpath is traveled by students of all ages, by rail fans, by photographers, and by hiking or picnicking families. One indication of its constant use is the issuance of several hundred patches and medals to Scouts who walk certain lengths of it. Many cyclists and horseback riders also enjoy parts of the route.

Problems such as improvement of the surface, bridging of a few streams and highways, and enforcement of rules, require the Board of fifteen directors to keep their 27-mile responsibility under constant surveillance. To lighten this burden, a small force of "security observers" was instituted, duly authorized by state and county police departments to report infractions of Path regulations.

In spite of old and new problems, however, the success of the Path has led to serious efforts to extend it into Kane County, to reach Elgin, Batavia, and Aurora. It is hoped that eventually an arrangement will be made with the DuPage and Kane County Forest Preserve Districts for protection and maintenance. Another long-range objective is to link up with other trails such as the "Fox Path" now being planned by a new group of land advocates in the Fox Valley north of Elgin. (See Appendix II.)

### 5. Thorn Creek Woods

Thirty miles south of Chicago's Loop is the bedroom suburb of Park Forest, the Valhalla of William H. Whyte's "Organization Man." According to Whyte, a distinguishing characteristic of Park Foresters is their propensity for community action, as symbolized in the legendary "koffeeklatsch." True to this tradition, a substantial group of Park Foresters, together with residents of neighboring areas, are today trying to preserve the feature for which their town presumably was named—a woodland belt covering some 1,000 acres, Thorn Creek Woods.

When Nathan Manilow and Philip Klutznick originally laid out Park Forest in 1948, they found two assets already in existence, the nearby commuter line of the Illinois Central Railroad and the Sauk Woods Preserve of the Cook County Forest Preserve District. The former promised accessibility to work, the latter to play. The Woods had been acquired by the District in 1917 with acute foresight of the population expansion to come a generation later.

While the power of the Cook County Forest Preserve District to buy land exists only within that county, nature itself is no respecter of political boundaries. Thorn Creek is a somewhat intermittent stream which meanders through the far south suburbs. From its headwaters in the cornfields of Will County east of Monee, it flows northeastward to join the Little Calumet River near Calumet City. Where it cuts through the Valparaiso Moraine, Thorn Creek has carved a pronounced ravine marked by steep slopes and further dissected by minute tributaries. The resulting landscape possesses remarkable topographical relief in contrast to the level outwash plain to the south.

Land near the Creek being too uneven for farming, the area has remained wooded. The woods north of the Cook County line comprise the Sauk Woods Forest Preserve. South of the line in Will County it is called "Thorn Creek Woods," approximately 800 acres of red and white oak and hickory forest mixed with white pine and other species planted in clearings.

Efforts to augment the area in public ownership began with a 1958 resolution by the Park Forest Village Trustees advocating that both the Cook and Will County Forest Preserve Districts purchase 250 acres of private wooded land. Cook County filled out its holdings in the area with the purchase of a 15-acre triangle on the county line. Will County did not respond.

In 1966, Bernard G. Cunningham, the president of Park Forest, issued a document entitled "Green Paper on Open Space." Essentially, the statement called for the use of extra-territorial zoning powers to designate 400 acres of Thorn Creek Woods open space. Upon the recording of a subdivision plat by a prospective developer, the Village would have a one-year option in which to purchase the land.

This enlightened attempt to make use of existing municipal powers was soon thwarted. Unwilling to abide with Park Forest's restrictions, developer Manilow, who owned much of Thorn Creek Woods, simply annexed his land to the village of Park Forest South, and zoned most of the woods for high rise apartments and expensive "estate type" homes. Since no governmental body seemed willing or able to reverse this decision in the interests of regional planning, survival of the Woods depended upon the intervention of private citizens.

Housewives Mary Lou Marzuki and Nancy McCrohon have become quite accustomed to smoke-filled rooms during the past three years. Their campaign to save the Woods has taken them, their husbands, and other members of the Thorn Creek Preservation Association, to innumerable public meetings, hearings, and caucuses in the local area, in the county seat, and in Springfield. They have also

Figure 12. Thorn Creek Woods, part of an 800-acre red and white oak woodland in northeastern Will County. Meadow in foreground will be developed within Park Forest South; the Village of Park Forest is in the background. Owl Lake, a glacial pond and slough, is at the near edge of the Woods with a plantation of white pine behind it. Photo by James Marzuki.

*Figure 13. Thorn Creek Woods. The trail leads into area owned jointly by the Village of Park Forest and the developer of Park Forest South. The proposed east-west freeway could obliterate this scene. Photo by Nancy Hays.*

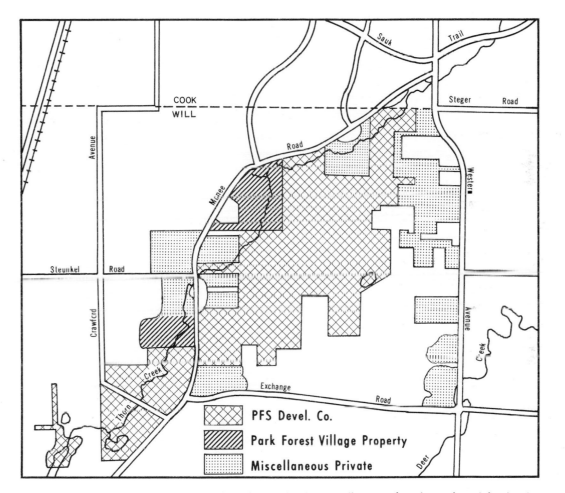

COOK
WILL

Sauk Trail

Steger Road

Avenue

Road

McKee

Western

Steunkel Road

Crawford

Avenue

Creek

Creek

Thorn

Exchange Road

Deer

| | PFS Devel. Co. |
| | Park Forest Village Property |
| | Miscellaneous Private |

*Figure 14. Property ownership in Thorn Creek Woods. This map illustrates the relationship of the developer's holdings to municipal and privately owned wooded land surrounding it.*

conducted conservationists, dignitaries, and public officials through the Woods itself, including the lieutenant governor of Illinois and both senatorial candidates during the 1970 campaign. Most visitors have pronounced it magnificent.

The objective of their activity is to persuade some governmental body to purchase the Woods for public use before it is destroyed or fragmented into home sites. According to its advocates, an expanse of woods in the midst of rapidly growing suburbs would constitute a multi-purpose open space of great importance. They point out the benefits from preserving the area: outdoor recreation, particularly hiking and picnicking; scenic relief; ground water replenishment; flood run-off; conservation education. (See Appendix IV.)

These benefits are, like Thorn Creek itself, scarcely confined to a single political jurisdiction. The populations of at least two counties and several municipalities would gain from the retention of the Woods. But this same spillover of benefits, together with the sheer quantity and value of the land involved, render it difficult for a single political body to undertake its purchase. The Thorn Creek Association therefore is attempting to weld a coalition of governmental agencies to undertake the project jointly.

Although the earlier overtures to the Will County Forest Preserve District went unheeded, a formal proposal was lodged in July 1969, that it should acquire the Woods, which would approximately double the District's present holdings of 1,100 acres. After this proposal had been tabled with the Real Estate Committee for several months, committee chairman John Francis in November 1969 proposed a resolution authorizing the District's first bond issue. Amid favorable comments about Thorn Creek Woods and open space generally, the motion to issue $1.5 million in land acquisition bonds was passed. The bonds were sold a month later at a favorable interest rate.

Meanwhile, land advocates Marzuki and McCrohon were in contact with the State Director of Conservation, William Rutherford. At the October meeting of the Conservation Advisory Council, they showed a ten-minute movie of the Woods together with detailed maps drawn by James Marzuki. Despite the presentation and a Department staff report favoring establishment of a "Thorn Creek State Park," however, it was decided to await local or county level action before State assistance would be provided.

Along with these efforts to obtain county and/or state action, the campaign was also carried to other parties controlling minor segments of the wooded area. The Village of Park Forest was asked to consider dedicating 124 acres which it controlled within the Woods. This was done by resolution of the Village Trustees. Another nearby segment slated to fall within the future campus of Governor's State University was designated by officials of that institution to remain untouched as an outdoor laboratory of ecology.

The Northeast Illinois Planning Commission in its review of the developer's application for federal "new town" assistance criticized his insufficient provision for open space, suggesting that the Department of Housing and Urban Development might require more open land as a condition to receiving federal aid. Thorn Creek may in fact prove to be a test case of the power of a regional planning authority to implement its will through review of applications for federal aid.

During the fall and winter months of 1969, the campaign to arouse the public continued unabated. Appearances at public meetings and guided tours through the Woods were undertaken by the half dozen principal members of the Association. One member, Mrs. Mary Brecce, took particular responsibility for covering meetings and maintaining good contacts with the press.

Essential to the effort was the excellent coverage provided by the local *Park Forest Star* and the county-wide paper, the *Joliet Herald-News*. The *Herald-News* put on special assignment a reporter who produced a steady flow of intelligent and detailed stories. The *Chicago Tribune* "South-Suburban Section" and the *Chicago Sun-Times* also carried the Thorn Creek story from time to time. Good coverage appeared even in *Chicago Today*, whose Day Managing Editor is the husband of one of the principal Thorn Creek advocates.

The effort to weld a state-county partnership to acquire the bulk of the Woods continued into 1970. A meeting in January brought together representatives of the State Department of Conservation, the Will County Forest Preserve District, Thorn Creek Preservation Association, and the Open Lands Project. No immediate agreement was reached; county and state each called on the other to make the first commitment.

A different route to state action on the Woods was initiated in a bill sponsored by Representative John Houlihan to authorize $3 million for acquisition of the State's share, by-passing the regular Conservation budget and providing funds earmarked solely for Thorn Creek Woods. The bill was passed in the State House of Representatives but died in the Senate Appropriations Committee. New bills have been introduced in the House and Senate.

Meanwhile, a new threat to the Woods was becoming apparent in the plans of the Illinois Division of Highways to construct a freeway through the natural area. It was learned that all planning studies for the road were being confined to a 1½-mile-wide strip, representing the south half of a "corridor" designated in 1962 by the Chicago Area Transportation Study. In an "Advisory Memorandum" issued in March 1970, the Open Lands Project attacked the wisdom and legality of limiting alternative routes to a strip which would inevitably penetrate the Woods, rather than looking at routes a mile or so south of the CATS corridor. (See Appendix I.) At the same time, the Northeast Illinois Planning Commission, which had designated the Woods as regional open space, informed the Division of Highways that NIPC would not approve an application for federal funds unless routes which by-passed the Woods were at least considered. In June 1970 the Chicago office of the State Division of Highways finally instructed its consultant to undertake studies of routes south of the 1962 corridor.

On July 1, 1970, the Department of Housing and Urban Development announced that Park Forest South had been designated as a "new town" under the New Communities Title of the Housing Act of 1968, the third project in the nation to so qualify. Under this designation, the developer would be entitled to federal loan guarantees on his debentures up to a total of $30 million. In addition, certain programs including open space preservation would be eligible for 70 percent rather than 50 percent federal participation. In exchange for such benefits, the development had to comply with a series of guidelines and standards set out for the program such as the following:

> Sec. 31.5(c) "It must have a favorable impact upon the growth and development of the area within which it is located in terms of conserving land . . ."
>
> Sec. 31.6(b) "Internal Development Plan. A new community must have a general plan and program for its ultimate development designed to create and maintain an attractive and viable environment responsive to human needs. Among the factors which the Secretary will consider in evaluating the plan are the following:

(3) Preservation and enhancement of natural features such as water bodies and steep slopes; establishment of an accessible open-space network for conservation, natural beauty, and recreation; and effectiveness of measures to prevent environmental pollution and problems such as flooding and soil instability."

Of particular interest to the conservation advocates was:

Sec. 31.6(e) "In those areas where there is an areawide planning agency certified by the Secretary, consistency must be found between the planning performed by the certified agency and the new community."

The Northeast Illinois Planning Commission at this writing is in the process of approving an open space plan designating Thorn Creek Woods as regional open space, which according to the Regulation must be respected by the developer.

In apparent conflict with the foregoing provisions, however, the developer released on July 21, 1970, a land use plan for Park Forest South, which called for the freeway and several clusters of apartments and estate homes to be built in the Woods.

Accordingly, the help of the federal government was sought to stop the planned encroachment upon the Woods. The Federal Council on Environmental Quality, established under the National Environmental Policy Act of 1969, took immediate interest in the problem as an opportunity to exercise an "ombudsman" role. The New Communities Division of HUD, alerted by the Council and by the Thorn Creek advocates, asked for a general meeting of all participants to clarify the points in issue.

On October 5, 1970, the HUD meeting was held at the developer's office with representatives from Open Lands, TCPA, Department of Conservation, NIPC, Will County Forest Preserve District, and the Nature Conservancy on hand. The developer stated his intention to adhere to his land use plan for the Woods; his main concern was that other abutting property owners would enjoy an unfair increment in vaue if his Woods were entirely preserved. TCPA and Open Lands responded that this did not exonerate the developer from his responsibilities under the federal regulations. In response to the developer's argument, several homeowners adjacent to the woods have signed statements indicating their intent to dedicate conservation easements to their own properties.

The general meeting resulted in the formation of an "ad hoc committee on Thorn Creek Woods," to be chaired by the Northeastern Illinois Planning Commission, which would attempt to define a mutually satisfactory boundary for a preservation area and a proposal for its acquisition.

The two meetings of the ad hoc committee in November and December 1970 at least promoted a sense of constructive harmony between the conservationists and the developer. Dr. George Ware of the Morton Arboretum was invited by NIPC to suggest a boundary for the most significant part of the Woods from an ecological standpoint. Ware's proposal embraced most of what the conservationists had sought, with some non-wooded buffer areas. It included approximately equal amounts of land owned or not owned by Manilow's Park Forest South Development Company. Presented by Lawrence Christmas of NIPC, the proposal was a masterpiece of ecological diplomacy.

The final outcome of the Thorn Creek story is unfortunately not complete as this book goes to press. The signs are favorable, however, for a happy ending. Support for the Woods continues to build. New bills are being introduced in the State Legislature to provide acquisition funds to the Department of Conservation, which presumably could lease the land to the adjacent Governor's State University for operation and maintenance. With respect to the South Suburban Freeway, a reorganization of the Chicago District of the Division of Highways has improved prospects for achieving a more enlightened route proposal.

Most important, the developer has stated that he will cooperate with any equitable solution. Hopefully, in retrospect it will turn out that the developer himself was the principal land advocate for Thorn Creek Woods.

## COMPARISON OF CASE STUDIES

The case studies call for some systematic comparison to distill the essential elements of land advocacy in practice. We begin with the dissimilarities.

Obviously each case differed from the others with respect to the size, character, and value of the land. Indeed the cases were deliberately selected to emphasize the different kinds of landforms and open space facilities which should be of concern to land advocates. Ecologically, they include a prairie, a tamarack bog, a slough, a deciduous forest, and a man-made right-of-way. They range in size from the 5.4 acres of Peacock Prairie to more than 800 acres in Thorn Creek Woods. They differed in value from an estimated figure of $11,500 for the Prospect Heights Slough to perhaps $3 million for Thorn Creek Woods.

The number of owners and governmental jurisdictions involved also varied from case to case. The prairie and the slough each was held by a single owner and fell within a single local jurisdiction, while Wilson Bog had several owners and overlapped two counties. Thorn Creek Woods had one major and several minor ownerships, and extended into more than one jurisdiction. The Prairie Path entailed fragmentary ownership and a plethora of jurisdictions along its 26-mile route.

Despite these apparently important differences, the case studies reflect a considerable similarity of problems encountered and solutions devised to meet each situation. As a preliminary generalization, it seems fair to say that the amount of effort required to preserve a piece of land is seldom proportionate to the size or value of the tract. One cannot assume that a small project such as saving the Prospect Heights Slough will be simple or quick; nor is there cause for despair at the enormity of other projects such as the Prairie Path or Thorn Creek Woods. Indeed we find a remarkable similarity in the effort, the attitudes, the burdens, and the rewards of the land advocates in each case, independent of physical and economic characteristics. Let us look at certain common aspects.

### Committee Organization

In every case except for the Prospect Heights Slough, a committee was formed with an official name, officers, and provision for membership. This preliminary step serves several obvious needs. First, it broadens the base of participation so that the initiators of the project do not have to bear the entire burden. (It is common, however, for the original land advocates to continue to do most of the work, albeit in the name of the committee.) Second, a committee structure affords a collective identity for purposes of publicity and sharing of blame as well as credit. Third, the committee can serve as an efficient vehicle for raising money, particularly if it is incorporated and receives tax-exempt status.

Three of the four citizen committees were eventually incorporated under the Illinois Not-for-Profit Corporation Act: Thorn Creek Preservation Association, The Illinois Prairie Path, and the Peacock Prairie Preservation Project. As described in chapter 4, the not-for-profit corporate structure is readily adaptable to the needs of ad hoc conservation activities. If the organization qualifies under Sec. 501(c)(3) of the Internal Revenue Code as a tax-exempt entity, contributions to the group are tax-deductible. Incorporation also adds formality to the structure of officers and members and helps to temper internecine differences of opinion on committee policy.

### Land Stewardship Appeals

As suggested at the outset of this chapter, the first resort of the land advocate ought to be to appeal to the conscience and common sense of the owner of the land in question. Land stewardship appeals of greater or lesser formality were attempted with respect to Peacock Prairie, the Prospect Heights Slough, and to certain owners in the Prairie Path and Thorn Creek situations. No attempt was made with Wilson Bog.

Obviously, these appeals were not very successful or the situations would not have become case studies of land advocacy. But Mr. McIntosh and Mr. Manilow at least tacitly cooperated to the extent that they did not precipitously exercise their rights of ownership in a manner inconsistent with the efforts to preserve Peacock Prairie and Thorn Creek Woods. Valuable time was thereby gained during which efforts to obtain public funds could be undertaken. The Prairie Path received several voluntary "license" agreements by which an owner permitted the public to cross his land, such permits being subject to revocation with a thirty-day notice. Since these permissions were extended without any payment required (except that the owners be held safe from liability), they are good examples of land stewardship.

### Zoning Challenges

The second recourse of the land advocate is to examine possibilities for use of the government's police power in keeping land open. Constitutional restraints upon the police power are such that it had no utility in the Peacock Prairie, Prairie Path, or Thorn Creek cases. The value of the land in each case was so great that an uncompensated prohibition against development would have been deemed an "unreasonable" deprivation of the owner's rights.

The Wilson Bog and Prospects Heights Slough situations, however, depended upon intervention in zoning proceedings. In each case, a petition of objection was circulated widely in the local community to be entered in the zoning proceedings.

### Public Acquisition Sought

In every case, some attempt was made to encourage public acquisition of the area in question. Such efforts ranged from the informal contacts of the Prospect Heights group with local Park District officials to the sustained campaigns on behalf of Thorn Creek Woods and Peacock Prairie waged at the local, county, state, and federal levels of government. In the case of Wilson Bog, since no local or county level open space bodies existed, contact was made with the State Department of Conservation which was already interested in acquiring a buffer zone around the nearby Volo Bog. With the Prairie Path, appeals to local governments were made for cooperation and limited contributions of services in kind, and DuPage County was asked for monetary and legal help in establishing clear title to the right-of-way.

### Scientific Evaluation

In every case except the Prospect Heights Slough, expert scientific evaluation of the area was procured to bolster the case for preservation. The Staff of the Morton Arboretum, the Illinois Nature Preserves Commission, the Nature Conservancy, and local university botanists such as Dr. Robert Betz of

Northeastern Illinois State College were helpful in different cases. Scientific testimony was usually valuable in both written form and in personal appearances at legislative hearings.

### Public Relations

Crucial to every land advocacy case was an active and vital public relations campaign. These efforts usually began with mimeographed "hand-out" materials describing the reasons for undertaking the project. Photographs, movies, and large maps were found to be valuable aids for use at public meetings and hearings. Talks before local school, church, civic, fraternal, and conservation groups were useful in spreading the cause.

As each land advocacy campaign reached a certain critical stage of "newsworthiness," press reports would begin to appear. The excellent press coverage given to the Peacock Prairie, Prairie Path, and Thorn Creek Woods cases depended in large part upon cultivating the interest of particular reporters and systematic feeding of information to key individuals. The degree of coverage accorded in the various kinds and levels of media—local, suburban, metropolitan, or national—varied according to the characteristics of the open space in question and the skill of the land advocates in "spreading the gospel."

### Success?

The degree of success achieved to date differs from case to case. Peacock Prairie may be regarded as a *fait accompli*; Prairie Path has about eight years left to run on its twelve-year lease; Wilson Bog and Prospect Heights Slough are temporarily safe pending their hoped-for acquisition by public authorities; and Thorn Creek Woods is still a cliff-hanger. But however varied the results, one common fact is uppermost: without the timely and continuing efforts of concerned citizens acting as land advocates, none of the open spaces would have been preserved.

Figure 15. Pine Rock Nature Preserve, a 59-acre tract several miles east of Oregon, Illinois, owned by Northern Illinois University. It will be held in perpetuity for scientific and educational purposes as a natural area. It contains an excellent stand of wet prairie vegetation with many unusual kinds of plants. Dry prairie, oak woodland, and a large outcropping of sandstone are also found in the area. Photo by Northern Illinois University Relations.

# 3
# LAND STEWARDSHIP: THE OWNER'S ROLE

## BURDENS ON PROPERTY OWNERSHIP

The ownership of private land in Illinois 1970 is quite a different matter from ownership in Illinois 1818 or Illinois 1900. According to tradition and the common law which Illinois derived from England, it could once be said:

> So great moreover is the regard of the law for private property, that it will not authorize the least violation of it; no, not even for the general good of the whole community. If a new road, for instance, were to be made through the grounds of a private person, it might perhaps be extensively beneficial to the public; but the law permits no man, or set of men, to do this without consent of the owner of the land.[15]

Consider quoting Blackstone to state highway officials or resisting payment of property taxes on the ground that they constitute infringement of the right to enjoy private property. Modern conditions have saddled the land owner with restraints, uncertainties and costs unimagined a century ago. Our society requires enormous amounts of land for public purposes, for roads, parks, schools, utility easements, municipal buildings. If such projects are legally approved by the voters or by officials responsible to them, then condemnation under the power of eminent domain is available to force a property owner to sell at a fair market value. Eminent domain is eminently constitutional, appearing in the Fifth Amendment of the United States Constitution, and expressed in some form in the constitution or statutes of every state.

Even where private land is not directly required for public purposes, its use can be regulated in many respects by public authority. Zoning, building codes, subdivision and floodplain regulations, and official map ordinances may be enacted by a county or an incorporated municipality. Such measures operate to limit the use of private land without compensation. As exercises of the public "police power" they must, however, be reasonably related to the protection of "peace, good order, morals, and health" of the community.[16]

When it comes to open spaces, zoning is a double-edged sword. To the extent that it serves the statutory function of "conserving the values of property," zoning may help to insulate open space areas from smoke, noise, or incompatible nearby development. On the other hand, its imposition on rural lands usually raises the assessed valuation, especially if they are zoned for commercial or industrial purposes. Thus taxes may be increased without any gain in revenue from the property.

The application and enforcement of zoning and subdivision regulations is highly localized in Illinois. Counties can enact zoning ordinances for unincorporated land within their territory.[17] Any incorporated municipality can regulate not only its own land area, but adjacent unincorporated land areas up to a mile and a half beyond its boundary.[18] Municipalities can also extend their jurisdiction by annexing contiguous unincorporated territory or incorporated areas where a majority of the residents so petition.[19] Thus the land owner who formerly may have been unaffected by land regulation except at the county level may suddenly find himself subject to the zoning policies of a burgeoning new municipality.

Aside from the owner's burden of land use regulations, his real property constitutes the primary source of local revenue. According to the Bureau of the Census, property taxation (including both real and personal property) accounts for 87 percent of all tax revenue for U.S. municipalities, having doubled in the last ten years.[20] State and local tax receipts rose *748 percent* between 1946 and 1967, a jump from 5.7 percent to 9.6 percent of the nation's gross national product.[21]

Rising taxes are frequently the *coup de grace* which makes further ownership of a piece of land unfeasible. Property in Illinois is assessed for tax purposes at "full valuation" as required in the State Constitution.[22] In practice, this value is measured by the "highest and best use" to which the property can be put. In a developing area, the maximum return from a piece of land is realized from growing houses rather than corn. Even though a land owner is willing to forego a developer's offer and desires to keep the land in its natural or agricultural condition, he is taxed at the level which would apply if the land were in fact subdivided. Such pressure is particularly applicable to flat midwestern land, readily convertible from crops to lots. The cost which an owner voluntarily assumes in choosing not to sell the land is thus augmented by public policy.

In urban fringe areas where soaring population requires constant improvement of schools, sewage, drainage, water distribution, and (one hopes) parks and forest preserves, property may be drastically revalued from time to time. After a quadrennial re-assessment, farm owners in DuPage County were required to pay about 250 percent more property taxes in 1967 than they were the year before.

Confronted with such a rising burden of taxes, municipal regulations, partial condemnation, and nuisance problems, the private land owner's only alternative frequently appears to be to sell. Civic responsibility and sentimentality aside, most land owners in developing areas simply cannot afford to retain what they own. Pragmatically, they sell their land, pay the capital gains tax, and reinvest the remainder in other ways. If they ever return to see their trees cut, their bog filled, their hills leveled, their creek culverted, and their fertile soil supporting crabgrass and concrete, one visit is usually one too many.

Ironically, the most valuable assets of land in its open state become liabilities to some developers, who buy land not because of its natural assets but in spite of them. Land values to such a developer are predominantly a function of location. He views the land simply as a volume into which to squeeze dwelling units; the nearer these dwellings will be to each other and to centers of employment, the more valuable is the "land space." Natural features which impede mass construction techniques or require artificial fill to make the ground capable of supporting houses actually lower the price he offers for the land.[23] Thus the owner who cares for these features may be doubly penalized: He becomes an accessory to the destruction of his natural landscape, and he receives a lower price than if it were flat and uninteresting.

While perhaps the most vocal lamentation over this dismal process has been raised by amateur conservationists and ordinary citizens, it has also attracted the careful attention of experts. Since the roots of the problem lie in real estate and tax law, it was necessary for a solution to be found through sophisticated legal techniques, rather than mere wringing of hands and howls of protests. The bibliography at the end of this book lists some of the products of this professional study. Their implications for the private owner are summarized in the following pages.

55

## THE GIFT OF LAND: TAX CONSIDERATIONS

The most direct means of preserving open land which the owner does not desire or cannot keep for his personal use is to donate it outright to a suitable public or tax-exempt organization capable of carrying out the donor's wishes. A gift of land may be the most rewarding single act of a person's lifetime.

While an owner's altruism may sometimes render possible tax benefits of secondary concern, there is no question that federal tax law can help to make land philanthropy more feasible. Subject to various restrictions designed to prevent abuse, it is clear that Congress intends that public spiritedness should be encouraged rather than hindered by the tax law.

The heart of the tax code dealing with charitable donations is Section 170 (a) (1):

There shall be allowed as a deduction any charitable contribution (as defined in subsection (c)) payment of which is made within the taxable year. A charitable contribution shall be allowable as a deduction only if verified under regulation prescribed by the Secretary or his delegate.[24]

Succeeding provisions of the code as well as specific regulations of the Internal Revenue Service provide guidelines for the treatment of individual transactions. Basically, the nature of the transaction is analyzed in the following steps:

1. Does the subject matter qualify for gift treatment?
2. Is it being "donated?"
3. Is the donation "charitable?"
4. What is the value of the property donated?

In the case of open land, no problem in answering the first question should arise: real property may be the subject of a gift just like money, securities, or other forms of valuable property. Even partial interests in land such as easements or remainder interests are legitimate subject matter for gifts. (See chapter 5.)

The question of donation depends essentially upon the intent of the donor, acceptance by a donee, and the finality of the act. If the use of the land is loaned subject to termination at will or is placed in a trust over which the former owner retains control, there is no donation. To qualify for the tax deduction, the commitment by the donor must be irrevocable. The only exception allowed is the inclusion of certain "watchdog provisions" designed to ensure that the purpose of the gift, i.e., the openness of land, will not be defeated through misuse or wrongdoing by the recipient. The main point is to recognize that the owner cannot later change his mind about a gift; only misconduct by the donee will bring a "watchdog provision" into play.

The question of "charitability" of a donation depends almost entirely upon whom the recipient is. The Tax Code and Regulations go into great detail with respect to qualified and non-qualified recipients. Basically, gifts are tax-deductible if made to the United States or any governmental subdivision thereof, or to a non-profit organization "organized and operated exclusively for religious, charitable, scientific, literary, or educational purposes or for the prevention of cruelty to children or animals." As a rule, any corporation, partnership, or sole proprietorship organized for profit is ineligible, as is any non-profit organization which engages in political lobbying.

If the proposed transaction clears all the foregoing hurdles, it is appropriate to consider what the amount of the deduction would be. For federal tax purposes, a charitable gift of land is valued at its present fair market value, i.e.. the value which would be paid by a willing buyer to a willing seller in the open market. As in eminent domain actions, the burden is upon the claimant to substantiate what he thinks the land is worth through expert appraisal and comparison with recent sales of similar land. Appraisal of unusual natural areas may be difficult owing to the lack of comparable land sales, but it is hoped that the Internal Revenue Service will recognize this problem and be lenient!

The deduction for charitable gifts which may be claimed in a single year is limited by the Tax Code. For an individual, the amount of the deduction allowed in the year of the gift is subject to an upper limit which depends both on the kind of property and the nature of the recipient. For gifts of land to a church, school, medical organization, governmental unit, or charity "substantially supported by the public," the ceiling on the contribution deduction is 30 percent of the donor's "contribution base."[25]

Gifts of land to certain kinds of "private" or "family" foundations which are not "substantially supported by the public" are deductible only up to 20 percent of contribution base.[26] (The limitation on charitable deductions for gifts made by a *corporation* is equal to 5 percent of its taxable income.[27] Corporate donations to entities controlled by the donor's controlling stockholder do not qualify as deductible.[28])

The difference in treatment between "30 percent" and "20 percent" donees is more significant with respect to the privilege of "carrying over" any unused portion of a gift for deduction in subsequent years. With gifts of land to the "30 percent donees" listed above, the unused balance of a deduction may be carried over to be applied against income during the next five years until exhausted.[29] In the case of "20 percent donees" however, the carryover privilege does not apply and the unused deduction is lost. For major gifts of land, therefore, the tax consequences may in part determine who would or would not be an appropriate recipient.

One way of coping with the limitations upon deduction of gifts to non-publicly supported organizations is to make annual contributions of an undivided fractional interest in the property. The amount of the fractional interest would be determined according to the size of donation which the donor could effectively deduct each year. In this way the greatest possible tax benefit is realized from a major contribution, even to a family foundation. However, the arrangement must clearly be a series of annual gifts, with separate paper-work for each. A single contract to make future gifts would be considered a single present gift divided into installments.

In the case of land whose value has appreciated greatly in the hands of the donor, the net after-tax cost of a donation (as compared with a sale) may be surprisingly low for a high-bracket taxpayer. The explanation is that the deduction for a donation of land is measured by its value at the date of the gift, rather than its original cost.[30] If the land is sold, a tax must be paid on "appreciation," the difference between the original acquisition cost and the sale price, which even at long-term capital gains rates runs as high as 25 percent. The saving of taxes due to deducting the appreciated value of the property as a *donation* may actually exceed the net proceeds of a *sale* remaining after payment of the capital gains tax. *It is sometimes better business to give than to sell!*

Mr. Peter Fritz, formerly on the staff of the Open Lands Project and now in the private practice of law, has worked out the following example of the operation of the tax deduction of gifts:

If your adjusted gross income is $40,000 and you make a gift of land to your county which cost you originally $12,000 but now has a fair market value at the time of the gift of $72,000, you may deduct 30 percent of your adjusted gross income, or $12,000, in the year in which the gift is made. This means you will be paying tax on only $28,000 instead of $40,000. Your tax saving is as follows:

| | |
|---|---|
| The tax on $40,000 would be | $14,400 |
| The tax on $28,000 would be | 8,600 |
| Your tax savings in the first year will be | 5,800 |
| You will save over the six years having carried forward the deduction | $34,800 |

In addition, you are relieved from paying a capital gain tax of $15,000 on the sale of the property. So the actual cost to the donor is $22,200 ($57,000 − $34,800), not $72,000.

The deduction for the current value of appreciated property is not a loophole uncovered by legalistic conservationists. Universities and other fund-raising organizations have long pressed its economic eloquence upon potential donors. Its terms apply to any gift of property, not merely to land, reflecting a Congressional intent to encourage charitable donations. Its use for preserving open space is highly appropriate and entirely ethical.

The outright donation of land may seem an idealistic gesture, noble in concept but rare in practice. But the New York Regional Plan Association estimates that one-third of public open space in the New York metropolitan area was acquired by donation. On a smaller scale, the conservation district program in Iowa has attracted many gifts, particularly of pieces of rough terrain that are otherwise unusable. And St. Louis, Missouri, is encouraging the donation of land in the form of "living memorials" to enhance its developing green belts.

In Illinois, many examples of donated open space may be found. The Morton Aboretum and the McGraw Wildlife Foundation were established through gifts of land by their respective owners to private foundations. Pilcher Park in Joliet was privately donated to that city. A strong possibility exists that 120 acres of virgin prairie in Chicago's southwest suburbs will soon be donated to a local university.

In nearby states, Wisconsin has received the tip of the Door Peninsula as a private gift; a Chicago physician has offered his summer retreat in Michigan for use as a nature study center. Indiana will soon gain a pristine remnant of the Valparaiso Moraine to be retained as a nature preserve.

Land set aside in building a "cluster development" may be the subject of a corporation charitable gift to a local public body.[31] (See Chapter 6.)

### PARTIAL GIFTS: "TO HALVE AND TO HOLD"

For most land owners, an outright gift of property, particularly of the family homestead, is out of the question. An understandable primary motive in wanting to preserve land is "selfish"—to enjoy it for one's own lifetime and perhaps pass it on to one's children. Such a selfish motive may actually be more consistent with the public interest than sale for development, yet in the usual case rising property taxes make retention of the land in its open condition prohibitively expensive. Both the private and the public interest may be best served, therefore, if the owner can be encouraged rather than hindered in following his natural inclinations.

But favoritism cannot be condoned even in the name of open land. Private property owners cannot be subsidized through property tax relief, income tax deductions or otherwise, without providing some quid pro quo in exchange. In order to gain favorable treatment *from* the public, the land owner must sacrifice something of value *to* the public. Fortunately, the ownership of real property entails many components of value which may not be recognized or needed by the owner, and may be the subject of partial gifts to the public.

Absolute ownership of real property, legally termed "fee simple," bestows a variety of powers, rights and duties upon the owner. The duties owed to the public and to other property owners have been discussed at the beginning of this chapter. Subject to those duties, the fee simple owner is entitled to occupy, exploit, and exclude the rest of the world from his land. The space to which his dominion applies extends both below and above the surface area demarked as his "property," and lasts indefinitely into the future.

Conceptually, at least, the fee simple domain is thus capable of being divided into these three dimensions: (1) in surface area by partitioning it into smaller parcels; (2) "vertically" by severing air or mineral rights or, for open space purposes, the right to develop the land; and (3) in time, by severing a leasehold, life interest, or future interest. Each of these methods of dividing the fee simple will be considered in detail.

### 1. Physical Partition

Donation of a fraction of his land is a simple and advantageous technique which many a land owner may never consider. Where a particular tract of land such as a woodlot or bog eminently deserves open space preservation and the owner does not wish to maintain it personally, that portion may be severed from the retained property and conveyed to an appropriate recipient.

The financial advantages of such an act are substantial. The donor may claim a charitable deduction amounting to the present value of the property contributed. And, of course, he ceases to be liable for property taxes on that tract. A gift of a portion of one's land may even be self-liquidating. It is a familiar fact in real estate circles that the presence of well-tended or natural open space makes property surrounding it more valuable. The owner of land adjacent to a preserve established by his own gift thus captures at least part of this increment in the enhanced value of his retained property. This effect has been demonstrated in the case of rights to stream valleys which have been donated to local open space commissions in Connecticut towns such as Litchfield.[32]

Aside from the possible financial advantages, the donor may in this way satisfy his conscience with respect to the land donated. Responsibility for the physical management and protection of the natural tract are shifted to presumably more experienced hands. In the case of a truly unusual piece of land, the knowledge that its preservation has been provided for should be as satisfying as ensuring the safety of other objects of one's responsibility and devotion.

## 2. Dedication of Development Rights ("Scenic Easements")

The Illinois Constitution, as stated earlier, requires that land be assessed for property tax purposes at full market value, based on the "highest and best use" to which the land can be put. In strict economic terms, private farms or other open land in the vicinity of an expanding urban area is most "valuable" as a site for housing, rather than in its existing use. Whether or not housing constitutes the "best" use for such land is a question of regional planning criteria. In practice, land capable of being developed is taxed as though it were in fact used for that purpose.

William H. Whyte in *The Last Landscape* states that until recently the assessors in most metropolitan areas have not adhered to the letter of the law: "If they had, some will tell you, they would have been run out of their communities long ago."[33] But Whyte goes on to point out that today new efficiency is being introduced into the assessment process. Suburban municipalities, strapped to finance new schools to educate the children of the new subdivisions, are forced to employ outside consultants to bring assessments into line. The huge revaluation of DuPage County farmlands in 1967 may be a reflection of such a new "hard line" policy.

Seven states have established preferential zoning for farm lands either by legislation or, where necessary, by constitutional amendment. Such measures generally require that farm land be assessed at its agricultural value, but in the event that it is sold for development, a prescribed penalty in the form of back taxes is imposed on the seller. Whyte, who originally advocated the concept, now feels that such provisions serve primarily to increase urban sprawl by facilitating speculation in well-located farm land, resulting in more distant land being developed first.[34] This particular device, in any case, is not presently available in Illinois; a bill passed by the Illinois Legislature to create agricultural zoning was vetoed by Governor Ogilvie in 1969.

The owner of Illinois farm land or other open land in the vicinity of growing cities, therefore, is liable for taxation on the developmental value of his land. For those who intend eventually to sell out for a developmental price, this liability is just. For those land owners who intend to retain their land in its existing use despite attractive offers from development, however, taxation of the developmental value makes fulfilling their intention almost prohibitively expensive.

The tax assessor obviously cannot differentiate between property owners on the basis of their subjective, even secret, intentions. But if the intention not to sell the land for development is made overt through a binding commitment, the assessor must take notice. Such a commitment can be made by irrevocably divesting oneself of the right to develop. Conveyance of the right to development through the device called a "scenic easement" or "conservation easement" gives the public or other recipient the power to prevent anyone from developing the land, the owner in particular. The owner retains the land itself and may continue to use it for rural or recreational purposes. He may sell it, but not for development. Neither he nor anyone else can develop the land once the development rights have been severed.

The obvious result of such an act is that the land becomes less valuable. Constitutionally, it can only be taxed at its *new* fair market value, namely as open land. Some states have passed statutes explicitly covering the situation in order to encourage such easements. But as Whyte points out, the issue is really a constitutional matter irrespective of legislation: "The very constitutional provision that assessors have followed to raise valuations now becomes the landowner's shield."[35]

Conveyance to the public ("dedication") of development rights to a property therefore should result in lower or at least static assessed valuation. However, certain pitfalls and a proposed solution are indicated in the following memorandum relating to Illinois Nature Preserves:

> A private owner who dedicates a nature preserve [one example of a "conservation easement"] might be giving up most if not practically all of the value of the property and therefore under the law the assessment might properly be for a nominal value or nil. However, there would be no exemption from taxes for the owner but only a reduction of the assessed valuation. While determinations of tax exemption are made by the Department of Revenue, determinations of assessments are made by the County Supervisor of assessments. Property is reassessed periodically and a satisfactory situation concerning the assessment of a nature preserve might change at some future time with a change of land values in the area or a change of point of view of the Supervisor of Assessments. If the dedicator owns land adjacent to the preserve and an assessment is made against the preserve land, this might possibly place an encumbrance on the adjacent property.

It appears from the above that a simple dedication of privately owned land as a nature preserve may not be satisfactory in some circumstances. A better procedure might be for the owner to dedicate the land with an instrument which also deeds the property to the State or some other public agency or charitable organization. This instrument could provide that the dedicator retains certain easements or rights or it could contain other provisions desired by the dedicator and acceptable to the State. Apparently such retained easements or right would not be considered as taxable property. There appears to be little in the statutes relating to the taxation of easements.[36]

Illinois does not presently have a general-purpose conservation easement statute. In its enabling statutes governing the operation of various open space public bodies, however, Illinois does permit the acquisition of interests less than fee. Specifically, the Department of Conservation,[37] County Conservation Districts,[38] and the Illinois Nature Preserves Commission[39] are authorized to accept easements. A general conservation easement statute has been suggested by the Illinois Planning & Conservation League at the time of this writing.

Generally speaking, if the conveyance of development rights takes the form of a charitable gift rather than a sale, the donor is entitled to a charitable deduction on his income tax. This was established by a specific Internal Revenue Service ruling on gifts of easements.[40] In rural areas the value of such a donation would be small; in urban areas it would approach the fair market value of the fee simple. It must, of course, be irrevocable to qualify as a charitable contribution.

### 3. Time Dispositions

### a. Future Interests

Many owners of land plan to continue to enjoy their property during their lifetime, and wish to ensure that it will remain open after their death. For various legal reasons, it is impossible to control the use of land by future owners indefinitely. It is entirely possible that heirs, or heirs of heirs, will eventually sell the land for development. Even when the progeny are wholly in agreement with the parents' wishes, the possibility remains that they will later have a change of heart or simply be unable to pay the taxes.

The family which strongly desires that land be preserved should consider making a donation of a "future interest" to a public or non-profit organization. Through the legal device of the future interest, ownership of the property automatically shifts to the public or non-profit recipient at the death of the donor or of the person whom he designates to have a "life estate" after his death. The heirs of the donor are relieved of paying inheritance or estate taxes on the land since they receive nothing, the property having been transferred independently of the estate.

Aside from the satisfaction of rendering a substantial public service, the donor may in certain cases be entitled to a *present* tax deduction for the value of the *future* gift. This deduction is calculated as the present fair market value of the property, reduced by the fair rental value for the number of years which the donor (and other life tenant, if any) is expected to live according to insurance-type life expectancy tables. In other words, the older the donor, the closer will the value of the tax deduction be to the total fair market value of the land.

The Internal Revenue Service no longer allows a present deduction for gifts of personal property, such as paintings, where possession would not vest until after the donor's death.[41] The Tax Reform Act of 1969 also restricted the privilege in the case of remainder gifts of real property. By special exception, however, the privilege remains in effect for a remainder interest gift of a "farm" or a "personal residence."[42] It is not yet known how broadly these terms will be construed; it is unlikely, however, that Congress intended to discourage gifts of natural land to the public.

An example of the use of the future interest donation is the program of gifts made by Mr. and Mrs. Edward L. Ryerson to the Lake County Forest Preserve District. In 1966 the Ryersons sold 87 acres of Des Plaines River bottomland to the district; the selling price in that transaction set the value for donations of adjoining land. In subsequent years the Ryersons have made future interest gifts of portions of their remaining land. The size of such gifts each year was determined by the amount of tax deduction they could take. In each case they have retained a life interest in the donated property.

### b. Future Interest Plus Development Rights

The donor of a future interest is not relieved of property taxes during his lifetime possessory estate since he retains the right to occupy and use the land. Therefore, it may be advisable to convey the development rights immediately to the ultimate recipient in order to reduce the property tax burden. Such complicated transactions must be adapted, of course, to the maximum income tax deduction which the donor can utilize. Even with the five year "carryover" provision, part of the deduction may be lost by contributing too much at one time.

### c. Term of Years

For younger land owners, a gift of a "future interest" would probably be ill-advised. The value of the gift for tax purposes would be negligible, and more important, the donors would be binding themselves and their children in a manner which might later prove to be premature.

A more cautious approach for a young couple who own preservable land is to convey the development rights, or full rights to part of the land, to a recipient for a definite term of years. If such a conveyance is in exchange for financial remuneration, income tax must be paid on the amounts received as rent. If the conveyance is gratuitous, the value of the interest conveyed may be treated as a charitable deduction when the public is clearly benefited. (It is unlikely that a non-permanent gift merely of development rights will be so considered.) Property taxes may possibly be stabilized or reduced during the term of effectiveness of the conveyance by arrangement with the local tax authorities.

The advantage of a term of years approach is that it permits a specific land-use plan to be attempted on an experimental basis, without permanently inhibiting the owner's property rights in case of failure.

### 4. Bargain Sales

An owner who can no longer retain his land may be unable to afford to make an outright gift, yet be equally unable to find anyone who will pay its fair market value and thereafter keep the land open.

In such a case he might consider making a "bargain sale" to a public or private land-holding agency, that is, selling it for the price which he originally paid for it. He is allowed to recover his original cost tax-free under current Internal Revenue Service regulations.[43] And he is credited with a contribution deduction amounting to the appreciation of the property he is donating. Depending upon his income bracket, the deduction may save him more money than what would remain after paying the capital gains tax if he were to sell the property at market value.

The "bargain sale" helps public agencies to cope with the high cost of land. Payment of at least original cost demonstrates an agency's good faith, while the gift of appreciated value stretches the public land acquisition dollar. In DuPage County, for instance, the William Greene family is employing the device in the conveyance of a 667-acre property to the DuPage County Forest Preserve District. One portion is being donated outright; the balance will be sold "at cost" with a gift of the appreciated value. The entire transaction is spread over several years and is calculated according to the family's tax position.

## SUMMARY

This chapter has attempted to describe three basic ways in which land may be preserved through voluntary sharing of property interests between the owner and some public or charitable agency. The owner's fee simple interest may be divided by transferring a physical portion of the land, by conveying the right to develop through a "conservation easement," or by severing a temporary or future interest in the property.

In practice, several of these methods may be combined to fulfill the owner's particular financial and personal interests. So diverse are the variables involved that it is impossible to catalogue all the possible "prescriptions" for land donation situations. In each case the decision must be reached by the individual owner and his family working with an attorney who is familiar with the various methods available. Conservation groups such as the Open Lands Project may be contacted for general assistance and encouragement!

Figure 16. Goose Lake Prairie was purchased in 1969 by the Illinois Department of Conservation, with the aid of $750,000 in private contributions raised by the Open Lands Project. Photo by Nancy Hays.

# 4

# WHO SHOULD HOLD OPEN LAND?

Once the best method has been chosen for preserving the land, the critical issue is where to find a suitable recipient for what is to be divested. A gift cannot be made unless it is accepted by some donee.

Obviously, the foremost criterion in such a selection must be reliability. Although any transfer of an interest in land for open space purposes must be hedged with legal safeguards, reliance upon the courts to carry out the owner's intent would be foolhardy. The recipient must be wholly satisfactory to the donor, both in its legal organization, its experience, and the personal attitudes of its officials. The only limitation is that the donee cannot be so amenable as to be the donor's "puppet." A "gift" for tax purposes requires a non-controlled recipient.

Charles Little of the New York Open Space Institute says that the best recipient is usually the most obvious one. In Illinois, the most obvious candidates are the various governmental activities concerned with the preservation of open land.

## PUBLIC OPEN SPACE PROGRAMS

The traditional method of preserving open space is the acquisition of appropriate land by a public authority. Governmental agencies at the federal, state, county and municipal levels are empowered to acquire and own land for public purposes. They may obtain it through negotiated purchase on the open market, through "condemnation" (forced sale), or through acceptance of donations or bequests. In certain cases they may also lease land.

Land so procured must serve some "public purpose" such as recreation, wildlife preserve, floodplain protection or preservation of a scenic view. It cannot be devoted to a purely private purpose, although private activities such as a yacht club may lease certain rights in public land or facilities.

## 1. Federal

Federal preservation of open land is conspicuous by its absence in Illinois. The national government owns no recreational or wildlife areas except in the extreme southern part of the state. Only recently has the federal capacity to preserve open land been felt in the Chicago region through the authorization of a National Lakeshore Park for remaining portions of the Indiana Dunes. The Department of the Interior is now studying a proposal for a lakeshore park north of Waukegan, extending into Wisconsin.

The main impact of the federal government in this area is through grants-in-aid to local open space agencies under the Title VII Open Lands Program of the Housing Act of 1961.[44] That statute authorizes the federal government to contribute up to 50 percent of the acquisition of open land for public recreation and conservation purposes. As of 1968, grants within the six-county Chicago region had been made to two forest preserve districts, eight park districts and two municipalities for the acquisition of more than 8,000 acres. The Land and Water Conservation Fund (Department of the Interior) provides similar assistance.

## 2. State

### a. Parks and Conservation Areas

Illinois's State Park System traditionally is ranked lowest in acres per capita among the 50 states in the nation. And the greater portion of state lands are located in the southern sections, far from Chicago and the mid-state centers of population. The Illinois Department of Conservation, which administers parks and conservation areas, had 189,490 acres under its management in 1966.[45] Only 13,848 acres of this total are located in the six-county area encompassing the Chicago region. According to the Northeast Illinois Planning Commission, as of 1960 fewer than 6,000 of those acres were developed as parkland in that region.[46]

Put another way, within 40 miles of downtown Chicago there are only three state parks, Illinois Beach (1,651 acres), Chain O'Lakes (960 acres), and Kankakee River (2,120 acres), and two

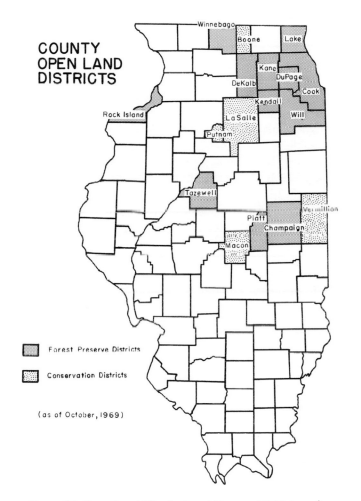

COUNTY
OPEN LAND
DISTRICTS

Winnebago
Boone
Lake
Kane
DuPage
DeKalb
Cook
Kendall
Rock Island
Will
LaSalle
Putnam

Tazewell

Vermillion
Piatt
Champaign
Macon

Forest Preserve Districts

Conservation Districts

(as of October, 1969)

Figure 17. Counties of Illinois, Forest Preserve Districts and
Conservation Districts.

"conservation areas" of 3,254 acres at Chain O'Lakes, and 580 acres at Wolf Lake in the shadow of Chicago's industrial belt. The three parks are well located from the standpoint of geography, being on the lakeshore to the north, the Valparaiso Moraine to the northwest, and the Kankakee Basin to the South. But their combined total of 4,731 acres is obviously inadequate to serve a metropolitan area of over 6 million people.

Most state park land has been acquired in rural areas where political and fiscal costs were low. Recently, however, the ability of the state to purchase for conservation purposes land which is simultaneously sought by industrial interests has been tested in the "Goose Lake Prairie" of Grundy County. Despite escalation in price due to competition for the land, the State Department of Conservation bought 1,800 acres of the Prairie in 1969. This may be considered a major victory of conservationists over politically astute industrial promoters.

While the state prefers not to purchase land in tracts of less than 1,000 acres, the Department of Conservation will accept gifts of smaller tracts. As of 1962, donated land amounted to 6,200 acres or about a fifth of Illinois's total.[47] These included gifts of *nine original park sites,* which were in most cases later rounded out through gifts and purchases. A good example of the catalytic effect of a gift was the establishment of the Kankakee State Park with a donation of only 30 acres by the Dummer family. Later additions to this core, especially by the Commonwealth Edison Company, boosted the park area to its current total of 2,120 acres.

### b. Nature Preserves

A different and quite effective way in which the state involves itself with open space preservation is through the Illinois Nature Preserves Commission. This agency is empowered to "inventory the natural land resources of the state, and to accept and supervise formal dedications of nature preserves in a system protected by stringent legal safeguards."[48] Either total or partial interests in property having significant natural qualities may be conveyed to the State upon approval by the Commission. The interest retained by the owner, if any, is enjoyed by him as private property subject to the preservation agreement he signs.

Since the property is declared by law to be put to its "highest and best use" in its state of natural preservation, the land is rendered almost untouchable by eminent domain proceedings for other public programs. The permission of both the Governor of Illinois and of the Nature Preserve Commission is required to condemn land so dedicated. Public as well as private lands may be protected from highway development in this way. The Cook County Forest Preserve District has so dedicated its most unique holdings.[19]

The Nature Preserves legislation in Illinois thus provides a convenient method for making gifts to the State of partial interests in land which qualifies under the statute. In cases of extremely desirable land, compensation may be paid for the interest conveyed at market or "bargain" evaluation. Where donation is made, federal income tax deduction may be taken for the value of the gift. The land would be subject to property tax assessment only at its lowered "fair market value" as open space, the right to develop having been severed. The owner would continue to enjoy the use of his premises, subject only to the self-imposed restrictions to which he is bound by his agreement with the state.

### 3. County

The most active level of government in the campaign to preserve Illinois open land is the county. Illinois law provides two kinds of county structures for the ownership of open land: the Forest Preserve District and the Conservation District. The voters of any county may establish one or the other, but not both.

### a. Forest Preserve Districts

The primary vehicle of past and present county-level open space preservation is the Forest Preserve District. Such districts have been created by the voters of ten counties, including five of the six counties of the Chicago region; McHenry voters have twice turned down a referendum to create one there.

The Cook County Forest Preserve District was created in 1916 at the urging of the famous pioneers of environmental planning, Daniel Burnham and Jens Jensen. Since then, it has made the county famous for its enlightened purchase and management of a belt of forests surrounding the city. The District now owns approximately 62,000 acres or 10 percent of the Cook County's land area. Under a recent referendum it has been permitted to expand to 75,000 acres. A major step toward this quota was the acquisition of 2,500 acres in northwestern Cook County in October 1968 for $11,035,000, the largest single land purchase in Cook County history.

A Forest Preserve District under its enabling legislation can hold land if it is forested or is capable of being re-forested.[50] The Cook County District, under the supervision of Charles "Cap" Sauers, has acquired much of the land best suited to forestation in Cook County. Two major chains of holdings occupy the bottomlands of two stream valleys, the DesPlaines and the North Branch of the Chicago River. Most of the remaining lands are located in the Valparaiso Moraine south and west of the Lake Plain. The largest cluster of preserves is at Palos Hills, situated atop a triangular morainic "island." Recent acquisitions are primarily of farm land which the District plans to reforest.

The pace at which a Forest Preserve District must operate is proportional to the imminence of its engulfment by urbanization. Cook County has long perceived this urgency and has nearly reached its statutory limit of land ownership. Five-sixths of all land held as forest preserves in Illinois are located in that county.

Just west of Cook, DuPage County experienced a doubling of its population in the decade 1950-1960. During the same period some 45 of the county's 331 square miles were added to the area already urbanized. By 1995 the present population of 313,000 is expected to grow to over 1 million. The county will be totally built-up except for pieces of land set aside by that time.[51]

Thus, the DuPage County Forest Preserve District has been operating under increasingly urgent conditions. In 1966 a formal study of the county's needs was performed by the Northeast Illinois Planning Commission under contract with the district. The NIPC Report recommended that the district's holdings at that time of 2,630 acres be augmented by acquisition of 10,357 additional acres.[52] Areas proposed for acquisition in the NIPC report were recommended chiefly in accordance with costs and site amenity. The proposed holdings would form a north-south chain along the west branch of the DuPage River in the western part of the county.

*Figure 18.  Winter lends a wilderness appearance to a Forest Preserve stream.*

As of July 1970, the DuPage County Forest Preserve District had acquired 8,000 acres toward a goal of 12,000 acres. Current plans call for the acquisition of nine areas, ranging from 10 to 550 acres in size, which would collectively require the entire funding capability of the District under existing legislation.[53] None of the tracts under consideration for purchase is in the eastern half of the county: land values are already too high in that rapidly developing sector. Even in the western region, DuPage has been paying an average of $10,800 per acre.[54]

Open land, however, has by no means vanished from eastern DuPage County, although this may not be true in ten years. Many farms and estates still exist in the "green wedges." Owners of such properties must choose between selling out to a developer and donating all or part of their land under a stewardship arrangement; the public simply cannot afford to pay the full development value.

Similarly, the Lake County Forest Preserve District is expanding its holdings in response to increasing pressure from population growth. As of July 1970, the Lake County Forest Preserve District owned 3,300 acres, with the acquisition of 560-acre McArthur Woods planned for 1971.

The focus of efforts in Lake County is the DesPlaines River Valley which extends from the Cook County border on the south to the Wisconsin line on the north. The District's hope is to establish a continuous chain of holdings providing 40 miles of hiking, bicycling, and picnicking facilities. A major link in the realization of this plan was the gift-sale (described on page 65) of 164 acres along the river by Edward L. Ryerson. Through the use of this technique, Mr. Ryerson is enabled to enjoy his home for the rest of his life at considerably reduced cost, and the county gains a substantial future holding in one of its most populous and most costly locations. The Ryerson gift has also inspired several other property owners along the DesPlaines to make donations to the Lake County Forest Preserve District.

Table 1 compares the progress of forest preserve districts in northeastern Illinois.

### b. Conservation Districts

The Conservation District was first authorized by Illinois statute in 1963.[55] The Illinois conservation district law was patterned on that of Iowa where the device has been highly successful.

TABLE 1.—*County Forest Preserve Districts, Northeast Illinois, Status Report, July 1970*

| | Cook | DuPage | Kane | Kendall | Lake | Will |
|---|---|---|---|---|---|---|
| District population | 5,640,000 | 495,000 | 260,000 | 30,000 | 375,000 | 245,000 |
| Acres owned | 61,900 | 8,000 | 1,385 | 201 | 3,300 | 1,050 |
| Acres per thousand pop. | 10.99 | 16.16 | 5.32 | 6.70 | 8.80 | 4.57 |
| Acres leased | none | 300 (from Atomic Energy Commission) | 160 | 10 | 510 (lease-back to sellers) | none |
| Potential indebtedness (without referendum) | $63,925,000 | $20,159,014 | $2,500,000 | not supplied | $16,000,000 | $5,500,000 |
| Actual present indebtedness | $36,925,000 | $15,110,000 | $1,100,000 | $19,000 | $2,847,938 | $1,500,000 |
| Approx. annual operating budget | $12,307,482 | $1,100,000 | $250,000 | $35,000 | $350,000 | $243,800 |
| Plans for future acquisitions | To complete statutory max.: 75,000 acres | 4,500 acres | 153 acres; looking for 200 more | As needed | 3 sites, 800 acres | not supplied |

Prepared by Rutherford H. Platt and Susan Burnam.

As many as five counties may jointly form a district to develop open space facilities on a large scale, but no county can have both a forest preserve and a conservation district. As described by the Illinois Comprehensive Plan for recreation development:

> In concept, it could provide a necessary means for an inter-county effort where open space within one county may be limited due to urbanization but where undeveloped potential exists in another county which lacks the funds for development. Also being a larger taxing and service district, it is better suited to meeting metropolitan regional park needs than the Forest Preserve District.[56]

Thus far, five Illinois counties have created conservation districts: Boone, LaSalle, Putnam, Vermilion, and Macon. Unfortunately, LaSalle's District was dissolved by referendum on November 30, 1970. Prior to that time, it had acquired 418 acres of prime natural acres through purchase and had leased an additional 302 acres, as well as 8½ miles of the Illinois and Michigan Canal. All these efforts, as well as a flourishing conservation education program, were erased by dissolution of the District.

### 4. Local

For smaller tracts amenable to recreational or educational purposes, a suitable recipient may sometimes be found at the local level: a park district, a school district, or a municipality itself.

### a. Park Districts

Illinois law authorizes the incorporation of park districts for the ownership and maintenance of recreation facilities at the local level. Districts may raise funds through bond issues outside a city's legal debt limit. Park district holdings, in contrast to forest preserves, are specifically oriented to recreation rather than conservation. And park districts may lease land for recreational use, whereas forest preserves must be acquired outright.

Some 200 park districts have been created in the State of Illinois since the concept became law in 1893. Their total holdings of 25,000 acres are estimated to increase by about 5 percent a year.[57]

In addition to land held by organized park districts, cities and villages are permitted to run park systems out of normal municipal revenues. Municipal parks not in park districts total about 5,000 acres in approximately 500 local systems. (For further information, contact the Illinois Association of Park Districts, 506 First National Bank Bldg., Springfield.)

### b. Historical or Special Areas

A donation of development rights—a "dedication"—may be made in certain cases under a 1963 statute relating to "Preservation of Historical and Other Special Areas."[58] The act applies to "areas, places, buildings, structures, works of art, and other objects having special historical, community or aesthetic interest or value." Preservation of such areas may be accomplished by dedicating the property to continuation of its existing use, either under the state law directly or under municipal ordinances establishing "landmarks commissions" pursuant to the statute. Experience in the use of the act is limited, but its applicability to certain kinds of open land properties is apparent. It explicitly provides for reduced tax assessment according to the value of the property in its preserved condition.

A major difficulty with saving land at the municipal level is that local politics raises its head. The primary credo of most municipal officials is protection of the tax base; any proposal which removes land from the tax role is likely to be viewed dimly. In the absence of state or county requirements that local open land be set aside, municipalities are frequently content to rely upon the forest preserves and state facilities to serve the outdoor needs of their residents. If the offer is one of development rights, local officials are especially prone to suspect a "tax dodge."

Unfortunately, land is immovable. The would-be land steward cannot threaten to pack up his property in order to get cooperation from local officials (or, in the exceptional case, to get away from unsympathetic neighbors). Even if the local government would not be a suitable recipient, the land owner should endeavor to enlist the support of the officials for his plan. Participation in local planning hearings and cultivation of the goodwill of leading citizens may prove to be vital to the success of the venture. Above all, the town must be impressed with the irrevocable nature of the sacrifice which the land owner proposes to make in order to achieve the preservation of open land. And it should be made clear that such preservation is in the interest both of the owner and of the municipality.

## PRIVATE RECIPIENTS

### 1. Charitable Foundations

If no public entity would be a suitable recipient, or if none can be found to accept the interest which the owner has decided to part with, he should then consider private organizations. Heading the list in Illinois would be the Nature Conservancy, a widely respected not-for-profit organization devoted to the preservation of natural areas. The Conservancy qualifies to own land in all 50 states and, in most, has been granted charitable tax-exempt status for property which it controls. In the past twelve years more than 150 different areas have been preserved by the Nature Conservancy.

Traditionally, the Nature Conservancy has been interested chiefly in land providing natural habitats for flora and fauna. Such lands it has either administered itself or conveyed under tight restrictions to another organization such as a forest preserve district or a university. Recently, however, the concern of the Nature Conservancy has broadened to include open farm land which is strategically located in rapidly urbanizing areas. Such properties are either purchased or accepted as a gift by the Conservancy, then conveyed to a local public authority for development for whatever open space use is most suitable.

The value of the Nature Conservancy, then, is to act as a responsible intermediate recipient pending decision about the ultimate use to be made of the premises. When time is short, owing to an unendurable rise in taxes or changes in family situation, land can be saved through donation to the Nature Conservancy which would otherwise fall to development. The Nature Conservancy also accepts gifts of future interests in land, and gifts of development rights, particularly from property adjoining land already under Nature Conservancy control.

*Figure 19. As substitutes for mountains in horizontal Illinois, some glacial erratics provide big challenges to small people.*

After the land has been conveyed to the ultimate user, the Nature Conservancy remains in the picture as a "watchdog," ready to repossess it if the user acts inconsistently with the open space purposes defined in the deed. This power is stipulated in a "reverter clause" in the deed with the recipient.

Other private organizations qualified to accept donations of private open land in Illinois include the Forest Park Foundation and the Open Lands Project. The Open Lands Project is in contact with all the organizations mentioned in this chapter and can serve as a "middle man" between donor and donee. Its office is at 53 W. Jackson Blvd., Chicago 60604.

Aside from organizations specifically devoted to the preservation of open land, there are an endless variety of organizations which the Internal Revenue Service qualifies as "charitable." Among these are universities and schools, both private and public, and religious organizations. Social service agencies such as the YMCA, the YWCA, the Boy Scouts, and the Salvation Army are also likely to be receptive to gifts of interests in land.

The only drawback to contributions of land to general service organizations is that they are in the business of performing a public service not necessarily related to the preservation of open space. Unless a piece of land is clearly designated as being conveyed for a limited purpose only, it may be regarded merely as a contribution of a disposable asset. Some organizations, for instance, view their holdings in the same way as securities and investments, to be held speculatively and sold at the most propitious time. Donations of land to these charities should be hedged with restrictions to a particular purpose such as a campsite, ball field, or outdoor environmental center.

## 2. Ad Hoc Open Space Entities

Where a land owner has a particular dream for his land and cannot find a public or charitable organization capable, willing, or trustworthy enough to undertake his plan, he may decide to create his own space entity. This may be done either on his own or in cooperation with like-minded neighbors. Such an ad hoc legal entity may take either of two forms: a corporation or a trust. Both are legally authorized to hold title to land and therefore may be set up expressly to accept a donation of open land and thereafter administer it.

### a. Not-For-Profit Corporations

A not-for-profit corporation may acquire land by gift, devise, or purchase.[59] Land in its possession may be administered, leased, donated, or sold, in accordance with the terms of the conveyance under which it received the property. The chief advantage of the corporate form is that perpetuation of administration is provided through a self-renewing board of directors. As with business corporations, the corporation itself and not the individuals responsible for its existence is liable for mishaps arising from the open space use of the land. Thus, a private owner may open his land to public use without incurring personal liability if he conveys it to a corporation of his creation. (Private owners of land in unincorporated areas who permit the public to enter the land for recreational purposes free of charge are safeguarded from personal liability under a new Illinois law.[60]

If the corporation is established to operate the land as a commercial enterprise, it would, of course, have to be a business corporation, rather than a not-for-profit corporation. In order to qualify for not-for-profit status, an organization must be limited to serving one or more of the following purposes: educational, religious, horticultural, social, or soil crop improvement. Clearly many sorts of non-commercial open lands schemes might qualify under one or more of these categories.

The not-for-profit corporation act greatly simplifies the procedure for creating and operating an open lands corporate entity.[61] No stock is issued or dividends paid by a not-for-profit corporation. "Members" are equivalent to "shareholders"; they elect a board of directors. A quorum at a directors' meeting can be as low as one third, and unlike a business corporation, directors may vote by mail. Requirements of notice for such meetings are minimal, and an annual members' meeting can be waived by written consent of a majority. Officers can be selected in any manner provided in the by-laws: theoretically, the former owner of the property can be president, vice president, secretary, and treasurer of his not-for-profit corporation.

The State requires only the filing of the articles of incorporation and the submission of an annual report on the affairs of the corporation. Fund raising, however, is carefully scrutinized, and the corporation can be dissolved for false solicitation.

### b. Trusts

Trusts are artificial creatures that take any form established by the trust instrument. Fundamentally, however, a trust must satisfy certain legal requirements: (1) the creator ("settlor") must have legal capacity to dispose of the property; (2) he must intend to create a trust; (3) the property concerned must be specific and ascertainable; (4) beneficiaries must be ascertainable; (5) the trustee should be specified; and (6) the purpose of the trust must be legal.[62]

The creation of an open land trust should raise no problem with the first three and last requirements. The fifth is dispensable since a court can appoint a trustee rather than let the trust fail. Although the designation of beneficiaries (4) may be impossible in the case of an open lands trust, the requirement does not apply to charitable trusts. And according to Russell L. Brenneman, the purpose of keeping open land in its natural state is likely to be a "charitable" purpose, thereby avoiding the necessity of choosing a specific beneficiary.[63] Another advantage of a charitable trust is that it may exist in perpetuity, whereas a non-charitable disposition is limited in duration by a complicated legal formula, "The Rule Against Perpetuities."

In Brenneman's view, therefore, the trust device "offers far and away the best method of achieving enduring and effective control over the future of . . . [open land]."[64] The only drawback is that the income tax deduction for charitable contributions does not apply to land placed in trust if the former owner retains the power to revoke the trust or reserves any interest in the property worth more than 5 percent of the total value of the land.[65]

In Connecticut and certain other eastern states, the use of a "land trust" for preserving open land locally is widely practiced. The Connecticut "land trust" is not to be confused with the Illinois creature of the same name. The latter is a special kind of trust which permits a bank or other trustee to hold title to land and protect the identity of the beneficiary. The Connecticut version is much closer to a non-profit corporation in its organization.[66] It is established under a state law and thus is strictly limited to the legislative provisions, in contrast to a trust which may take any form. The trust is also subject to a set of by-laws and is administered by a board of trustees. It functions as a public landholding agency; it is most useful as a recipient for donations of scenic easements along a stream, a ridge, or some other geographically extensive open space amenity. For Illinois, the not-for-profit corporation serves these purposes admirably.

*Figure 20.* Illinois's oldest known tree was this thousand-year-old cedar which overhung the gorge of the lower Fox River until cut down by vandals in 1968. Photo by Dick Young.

# 5

# HOW TO KEEP OPEN LAND OPEN

Once the property owner has decided how to "pare down" his ownership rights most advantageously and has located or created an entity which will accept a donation of the land, development rights, or future interest to be severed, it is essential to convey it with legal safeguards against misuse. The most obvious misuse to prevent would be any action by the recipient which compromises the open character of the land, such as the cutting of timber or the sale of development rights to a builder.

Confidence in the present good faith and reliability of a recipient is no reason to avoid the problem of legal safeguards. Regardless of the degree of confidence which the donor feels toward the recipient, he (and certainly his lawyer) must take the long view. Individuals change jobs, lose interest, move away, or die. Circumstances change, such as the way surrounding land is used. The open space preservation scheme, therefore, must be a creature of law, not merely of personal trust. The responsibilities of the recipient must be clearly defined and provision made for "policing" of its actions, and substitution of another agency or organization if required.

The instrument of conveyance must provide that the holder of the open space interest would be replaced in time to prevent damage to the premises. Such a provision would constitute a permanent restriction on the title to the land, something which the law traditionally abhors.

## LEGAL RESTRAINTS ON "DEAD HAND" CONTROL

It might be ideal if the present land owner could impose his wishes concerning his land through a legal instrument which would be binding on everyone thenceforward and forever. But the law does not so allow. The courts are traditionally hostile to the encumbering of the free use and enjoyment of land through "dead hand" restrictions. The public interest is believed to lie in the free marketability of land, a concept directly opposed to the restriction of land to open space purposes, even where a public benefit is intended. This judicial attitude is backed up by certain rules and statutes, both ancient and modern, which constitute hazards for any attempt to preserve the openness of land indefinitely into the future.

### 1. The Rule Against Perpetuities

The hoariest of the legal doctrines which seek to prevent "dead hand" control of property ownership is the Rule Against Perpetuities. Derived from early English common law, the Rule provides that "no interest in property is good unless it must vest, if at all, not later than 21 years after some life or lives in being at the time of creation of the interest."[67] Exact interpretation of this rule can be left to harassed law students and those practitioners who need it. Fortunately for purposes of open land planning, there are several instances where the rule definitely does not apply. The discussion that follows will focus on those exceptions. The main point here is that an open lands arrangement must be drafted by an attorney with a wary eye on the Rule Against Perpetuities. If the rule is violated at the outset, the legal safeguards installed in the plan will not operate.

### 2. Merchantable Title Act

A new legal device intended to free real property from stale restrictions is the "marketability statute" passed in Illinois and several other states. Under the 1959 "Merchantable Title Act"[68] any claim or interest in land held by someone other than the owner is valid for only forty years from the time it arises. In order to preserve such a claim or interest, a "statement of claim" must be filed with the County Recorder of Deeds where the land is located at least every forty years.

In other words, a prospective purchaser of land need only search his record of title back in time for forty years. Any outstanding interest not revealed through a "statement of claim" recorded within forty years may not be asserted against an owner who has a clear title extending that long.

The statute does not apply to interests readily ascertainable from an inspection of the premises, such as someone in possession or a visible easement such as a private road or a utility line. Open space restrictions probably would not be saved by this exception, however, since it is doubtful that the existence of a right to enforce the open character of land would be readily apparent from inspection.

One of the duties of the holder of an interest in open land, therefore, must be to file the required "statement of claim" at timely intervals. Not to do so would be to risk forfeiture of its open character. The instrument of conveyance to the recipient must, therefore, provide for replacement of the holder upon his failure to perform this duty.

### 3. "Doctrine of Changed Circumstances"

Another expression of the judicial attitude against dead hand control of real property is the "doctrine of changed circumstances," under which the courts upon petition by the owner of land burdened with old restrictions (particularly covenants) may examine changes in the use of surrounding real estate to determine whether restrictions should be removed. Open space restriction should be recognized as intended to operate in the face of changes in neighboring land use. But as in relation to the Merchantable Title Act, a positive duty must be imposed upon the holder of the open space interest to defend it against challenge under the doctrine of changed circumstances. Like a failure to file a statement of claim, a failure to defend the restricted use would amount to forfeiture of the openness of the land. Therefore, a duty to defend must also be spelled out in the instrument conveying the interest.

### LEGAL TOOLS FOR EFFECTING DONOR'S WISHES

Having mentioned the needs and problems connected with the use of legal safeguards, it is appropriate to examine the array of legal devices available for such a purpose. Although the legal arsenal is limited both in number of weapons and experience in their use for open space purposes, the devices themselves are long familiar to Anglo-American law, and there have been successful tests in many states.

### 1. Reversionary Interests

To begin with the least usable technique, land may be conveyed subject to a requirement that it perpetually be used for open space purposes or with specific prohibitions against cutting trees and the like. The instrument of conveyance may provide that in the event the restriction is broken, the "grantor" or original owner will be entitled to enter and take over the property. After the conveyance is made, but before the restriction has been violated, the grantor retains only one interest in the property, the power to enforce the restriction by recovering the land. If he will automatically become owner again upon breach of the restriction, he is said to own a "possibility of reverter." If such reversion is not automatic but would require him to go to court to regain ownership, his interest is called a "power of termination." In either case, his retained interest exists only as a future contingency, not entitling him to any of the rights of ownership unless and until the condition is broken.

One drawback to the use of these "future interests" is that Illinois law regards them as strictly personal interests. The individual holding them may not sell, donate, or devise them in a will.[69] They survive his death only through inheritance by the heirs to his real property. If held by a trust, such rights cannot be transferred, except to the beneficiaries at the trust's termination.[70] If held by a corporation, they cease entirely if the corporation is dissolved.[71]

The efficiency of the power of termination and the possibility of reverter then is limited to cases where transfer to one's heirs or to the beneficiaries of a trust is the intended mode of disposition. Another weakness renders them even less effective for any open space goals. Although both interests are historically exempted from the Rule Against Perpetuities, an Illinois statute limits their duration to forty years.[72] This is a different statute from the Merchantable Title Act: these particular interests may not be preserved through filing a periodic statement of claim. They are simply cut off by law forty years after their creation. The power of termination and the possibility of reverter would not protect open land after that period.

### 2. Executory Interests

A variation of the foregoing theme is to name a party other than the original owner to take over the land upon breach of an open space restriction. This seemingly insignificant provision makes a great difference in law. The power in a third party to seize ownership upon the happening of a stated contingency is called an "executory interest."

Unlike the power reserved to the grantor himself, the executory interest is not cut off peremptorily by Illinois statute (although presumably the Merchantable Title Act would require it to be preserved through periodic filing). However, the executory interest is subject to the Rule Against Perpetuities.[73] To be effective, therefore, it generally must be limited to the length of time permitted by the rule's magic formula: "life or lives in being plus twenty-one years." An attempt to protect an executory interest farther into the future than allowed by the Rule Against Perpetuities is totally ineffective from the beginning. So tricky is that rule that the safer course would seem to be to avoid using the executory interest technique in the first place.

Fortunately, however, an exception exists which allows the executory interest to be used in a most effective way. We have indicated that a "charitable trust" unlike an ordinary trust is exempted from the necessity of naming a beneficiary and is permitted to exist in perpetuity. The same favoritism toward charity is found in the law of executory interests. According to both Dunham[74] and Brenneman,[75] a donation which is protected by an executory interest placed in a second charitable (or public) entity is valid, even though the latter interest might vest after the expiration of the period permitted by the Rule Against Perpetuities. Thus a gift to a park district subject to an executory interest in a conservation organization serving as "watchdog" is valid.

### LEASES

The foregoing discussion has related to conveyances of *fee simple* interest in land subject to an open lands restriction. If, instead, the interest is conveyed only for a term of years under a lease, a different result occurs. The lessor may retain not only the right to re-enter at the end of the term, but also may reserve a power to terminate the lease in the event that an open space restriction contained in the lease is broken.

Such a right of entry retained by a lessor is specifically excluded from the statute limiting powers of termination and possibilities of reverters to forty years. It does not matter how closely the length of the lease term approximates a permanent interest. If the interest is conveyed for 999 years, the lessor's right of entry if a condition is broken is not cut off; but if no term is stated, the conveyance is one of the fee simple, not a lease, and a retained right of entry lasts only forty years. Even re-filing will not extend the term.

## COVENANTS AND EASEMENTS

The effectiveness of open land protection is greatly enhanced where the party concerned with its preservation owns land adjacent ("appurtenant") to it. Such a situation arises where a land owner conveys his marsh or woods to a public entity while retaining other contiguous property for his own use. In such a case he may impose a covenant or an easement upon the conveyed land requiring that it be kept in a natural condition, with no timber cut, no ponds filled, and other limitations.

Such an easement or covenant is said to "benefit" his retained land by rendering it more valuable. Where such benefit to appurtenant land exists, the owner of the benefited land and his successors may enforce the restriction against not only the immediate owner of the open ("burdened") land, but against his successors as well. Thus the land remains subject to the restriction even though sold or inherited.

Where the power to safeguard open land belongs to one who does not possess property appurtenant to the open land, the law becomes more uncertain. In such a case, no land is benefited; the benefit runs only to the holder of the interest personally. He is said to have an easement or a covenant "in gross" rather than "appurtenant." The holder of an interest in gross may enforce the open space restriction only against the immediate owner, not against his successors. Without appurtenance, the restriction does not "run with the land."

An easement or covenant in gross would arise where a property owner conveys an entire parcel subject to an open land easement or covenant, without retaining any contiguous land to be benefited by that retained interest. So also, when development rights alone are conveyed by an easement to some public or charitable organization which has no property next to the land to be preserved, that organization holds the easement "in gross."

The reasons why an appurtenant interest is preferable to one in gross are beyond the scope of this discussion. Easement and covenants in gross are enforceable between the original parties to a conveyance. Difficulty only arises where one or both of the original parties has been replaced by a "successor."

Neither a covenant nor an easement is subject to the Rule Against Perpetuities. Both are presumed to be subject to the Merchantable Title Act, although easements "visible upon inspection" are not subject to the filing requirement.

The technical difference between an easement and a covenant is simply that the former is an interest in real property, whereas a covenant is merely a contractural agreement as to the use of land. For this reason a covenant may be invalidated at some future time if the holder of the land proves to a court that the agreement is no longer reasonable in the light of "changed circumstances." As an interest in property, an easement cannot be challenged in this way; reasonable or not, it exists until the party enjoying its benefit causes it to end or it is abandoned. But, even a covenant should be capable of withstanding an attack on its "reasonableness" if it is properly drafted to make clear that the restriction on open land is intended to operate in the face of "changed circumstances."

It should also be specified that enforcement of either form of restriction will take the form of injunction to prevent physical damage to the premises, rather than merely money damages. A covenant which can be enforced through an injunction is called an "equitable servitude," which is virtually the same thing as an easement. The confusion in terminology is of no importance if the message is clear!

*Figure 21. The Nadelhoffer farm and the two halves of Woodridge in DuPage County. The woods and marsh which would be preserved through planned unit development is at upper left. Photo by the author.*

**6**

# WORKING WITH THE DEVELOPER

We have considered the role of the "land advocate" in defending open space owned by someone else and the role of the "land steward" in preserving his own property. But many a property owner is compelled to sell for development yet still wants to protect the best qualities of the land.

For one reason or another, the "partial gift" solutions outlined in the last chapters may be unsatisfactory in individual cases. The owner may have insufficient current income to take advantage of a sizeable tax deduction, or he may need maximum proceeds from selling the property, or perhaps no suitable donee can be found. In any event, the decision to sell for development does not necessarily foreclose the owner's ability to influence what is done with the land. Assuming a seller's market, which exists for well-located land even during periods of "tight money," the owner is in a position to attach strings to his sale or to select a developer whose philosophy is consistent with his own.

The important fact for the owner to realize is that there are more ways than one to develop land for residential use, and the profit to be realized is not necessarily proportional to the acreage which is bulldozed. Some background information on the growing popularity of "open space communities" is appropriate, to be followed by a case study illustrating the proposed use of such techniques in DuPage County, Illinois.

## THE POST-WAR LEGACY

If the motto of the Thirties was "a chicken in every pot," its sequel in the post-war Forties and Fifties might have been "a house on every lot." The combination of a national sense of gratitude to members of the armed forces and an unprecedented national prosperity spawned a house-building era unequalled in history. Fueled by federal mortgage guarantees provided through the Federal Housing Administration and the Veterans Administration, most of this activity was directed to the construction of single-family homes outside the central cities.

The entrepreneurs who implemented this wave of building, Levitt, Manilow, Klutznick, et al., essentially created a new urban form which was to become standard across the country. In contrast with older communities oriented to public transit systems and commuter railroads, the new subdivisions were oriented to the automobile. Location within the community became irrelevant to value, since any resident could reach a shopping center, school, or expressway access with almost equal convenience. Developers were therefore motivated to obtain as much land as possible and to develop it with single-family homes as thoroughly as possible.

Zoning during the Forties and Fifties was inadequate to the task of harmonizing development with the natural environment. Local ordinances were directed primarily to the segregation of use districts, residential, commercial, and industrial, and to restraints on "bulk" as reflected in the size of the house in proportion to its lot. It was emphatically not an objective of the zoning process to attempt to relate the location or character of development to the physical features of the land. Even in cases of obvious physical hazard such as floodplains or slopes subject to mudslides, there was great reluctance to employ zoning powers to limit development.

On the contrary, zoning actually contributed to urban sprawl. Requirements which established uniform lot size, set-back, and density became physically embodied in the dreary monotony which characterized post-war suburban development. In a token bow to the Garden City ideal, streets were frequently curved and terminated in cul-de-sacs. Yet with no differentiable open spaces or interesting places reserved from development, such attempts at variety simply emphasized the sameness of the giant subdivisions.

Recognizing that zoning policies, along with FHA requirements and land economics, were important determinants of the urban sprawl of the 1950s, concerned leaders have given considerable attention to the problem of making zoning more responsive to environmental realities. Constitutional difficulties are inherent to such efforts: "spot zoning" or restrictions applicable to individual parcels of land are not permissible. Whatever privileges or impediments are bestowed under the zoning power, they must be generally available to all property owners in a similar situation. Otherwise, "equal protection of the law" is violated.

## NEW INCENTIVES FOR OPEN SPACE

The solution which has proven most effective in various applications is to create incentives for the developer to keep certain land undeveloped. Open space does not *per se* earn an economic return for the developer who protects it. It is appropriate, therefore, for the local planning authorities to permit a higher return from development of the remaining land than would otherwise be obtainable. They can accomplish this by permitting greater than usual density on built-up land in exchange for the preservation of a certain percentage of open space.

In downtown business districts, this principle is applied through relaxation of maximum height restrictions for new office buildings which provide an open plaza at street level. The new First National Bank Building and the John Hancock Center were both constructed under such an incentive provision in the Chicago Zoning Ordinance.

### 1. Cluster Zoning

For suburban development, the analogous technique is called "cluster zoning." Under a clustering provision, no more dwelling units are necessarily permitted in a given land area than under traditional zoning, but they may be built closer together. By grouping residential units in rowhouses, garden apartments, or separate homes with smaller private yards, land is spared which may be kept for community open space. In carefully planned developments the land retained in open space is deliberately selected for its special natural characteristics or suitability for outdoor recreation.[76]

The developer is likely to gain in two ways from cluster zoning. First, by placing his homes closer together, they may be served by a less extensive system of utility lines, streets, sidewalks, and sewers. The fixed capital investment needed to serve a given number of homes is therefore decreased without any corresponding decrease in selling price. Second, the presence of community open space is likely to enhance the value of homes in the vicinity. Although private yard areas are smaller in cluster developments than in conventional subdivisions, homes may command a premium price by virtue of

97

having access to more spacious community land. According to an Urban Land Institute study by Carl Norcross, home-buyers are indeed attracted to cluster developments.[77]

### 2. Planned Unit Development

A more elaborate application of the incentive principle is the device known as "Planned Unit Development" (PUD). A PUD involves not merely a relaxation of the zoning requirements for density, but the drafting of a whole new "rulebook" to cover the tract in question. The opportunity to qualify for PUD status is created through an enabling ordinance in the municipality or county which sets out requirements as to size of development, standards of design, land use, open space, over-all density, parking, and community facilities.

In order to qualify, a developer must file with the appropriate local governing body a detailed application which demonstrates his compliance with the enabling ordinance. If deemed to be satisfactory, the application itself is passed as an ordinance and recorded as a legal PUD. Thereafter, the developer must obtain an amending ordinance should he wish to depart from the provisions of the accepted plan.

The PUD thus incorporates cluster zoning to obtain open space and also offers flexibility in other aspects of community development such as mixture of house-types and of residential and commercial uses. An unpublished report by the Northeast Illinois Planning Commission states:

> Planned unit development is an increasingly popular way to encourage flexibility in development for the benefit of both community and the developer. The aim is to produce a residential environment which reflects ingenuity, imagination, and design efforts on the part of the builders, architects, site planners, and developers, and which allows amenities to the residents of the planned unit development not possible under traditional zoning.

In the case of either PUD or a cluster subdivision, the question arises of what should be done with the retained open space. Once dedicated on a plat or plan which is officially recorded, the open space is legally safe from development, yet presents a problem of continuing maintenance, payment of taxes, and administration of use. Except in rental developments, the builder normally wants to get out of the picture as soon as possible. He certainly does not want to assume the role of perpetual custodian of community open spaces. Like the property owner in the preceding chapter, the developer must find or create a recipient to whom the land may be transferred.

The public open space agencies described in Chapter 4 provide some possibilities. Wooded areas may be accepted by the county forest preserve district; playground and other recreation areas might logically be conveyed to the local park district. In either case, administration is placed in professional hands and the land is removed from the tax roll. In such dispositions, the use of the land is, of course, open to the general public.

If transfer to a public body is unfeasible, the usual way of providing for open space management within a development is to create a homeowners' association, with membership bestowed automatically upon every purchaser or tenant. When established as a not-for-profit corporation, the association may take title to the land. Thereafter, taxes, development, and maintenance of facilities are financed out of assessments levied by the association upon its members, in accordance with a contract which each member signs upon his occupancy of a home in the development.

PUD enabling ordinances are recent innovations in many Illinois municipalities and counties; experience in their use is sparse. Lake County, for instance, was placing the finishing touches on its new PUD ordinance when a developer submitted a plan which would have jeopardized the state-owned Volo Bog preserve. Approval was granted under the conventional zoning law, subject to the unusual condition that the developer return with a PUD application when the ordinance was completed. Clearly, the chances for safeguarding the bog would be improved under the more flexible provisions of Planned Unit Development.

To return to the owner's role, the existence of a PUD enabling ordinance or a cluster provision in the local law affords a great opportunity to a property owner to affect the future development of his land. At very least, he can include a covenant in his contract of sale that the purchaser-developer shall apply for PUD status and shall accordingly maintain a certain proportion of open space. In cases where the owner wishes to remain in the picture, he may reserve a contractual right to review and veto the plans of the developer. Of course, if this veto privilege is made completely arbitrary despite considerable investment by the developer in planning services, he may not find any takers. Some arrangement for mutual collaboration and arbitration by an impartial third party would probably be necessary.

In the case of maximum participation by the owner, short of becoming his own developer, he may enter into a partnership or joint venture with a development firm. Such a status gives him a share in the control and planning of the enterprise to the extent of his proportion of the partnership. In place of an outright price for the land, he shares *pro rata* in the gains (or losses) of the project. In this way he may experience direct economic benefits from his concern for safeguarding open space areas.

While such a level of involvement by a property owner in the development of his land is unusual, it is not unthinkable. The following case study from DuPage County, Illinois, recounts how a group of property owners, even though compelled to sell for development, is going to every length to protect the best features of their land.

### Case 6. The Nadelhoffer Farm

The six-year-old bedroom suburb of Woodridge, Illinois, is shaped like a dumbbell. The two "weights" at either end consist of subdivisions housing a total of 13,000 persons. The connecting "handle" is a strip of land a hundred yards wide and about a quarter-mile long which provides the "contiguity" required by Illinois law for territories to be annexed to one another in a single municipality.

Lying between the two halves of Woodridge and transected by the annexation corridor is a vestige of DuPage County's rural past: the 178-acre Nadelhoffer farm. With one border of the property angled to conform with the Indian Boundary of 1816 and other borders lined solidly with the suburban homes of Woodridge, the property is a bridge in time as well as in space.

Topographically, the farm lies in the midst of the Valparaiso (or Wheaton) Moraine. The northern half of the property is a fertile upland which slopes down toward a marsh and a small creek in the southern half. About 80 acres around the marsh are covered by oak-hickory woods of virgin quality. The surrounding area in directions other than Woodridge is rolling farmland, with occasional English-style copses marking depressions and the courses of creeks. Horses still graze in some fields. Coveys of pheasant burst from cover at the approach of a human being.

The Nadelhoffer farm is no gentleman's tax shelter. It has been in the family for one hundred years through five generations. Twice in its day, the farm had the highest producing herd of cows in Illinois. The father of the present occupants introduced alfalfa into DuPage County in the early Thirties and was a keen advocate of "grassland farming" and "minimum tillage." Although crops are still grown here, the revenue from farming today amounts to less than the cost of taxes, not to mention the interest which the value of the property would be earning if otherwise invested. Farming is no longer an economic proposition in central DuPage County, 30 miles from Chicago.

The ownership of the farm is split among seven principal descendants, most living in other parts of the country. Since none of the co-owners is particularly wealthy and most have children, the possibility of donating the property for open space use is not practical. The family needs the proceeds of a sale at market value—that is, the development price.

In most land sale situations, there would be nothing more to write about. The family homestead would be regretfully conveyed and the proceeds happily reinvested. The land would be cleared and that would be that.

The departure of this case from the normal pattern is attributable to the environmental interests of the farm's owners-in-residence, Herb and Julie Nadelhoffer. In contrast to their 13,000 immediate neighbors to the west, north, and south, this couple is rooted deeply in the land on which they live. Herb and his brother Carleton, an attorney, were born and raised on the farm, and Julie comes from a Southern Illinois farm family. They understand soil and drainage, growing seasons, horses and manure, wildlife, ecology, and lilacs in the dooryard. As heavy construction equipment hurtles over the recently paved county road called 71st Street and fumes waft on an easterly wind from the Metropolitan Sanitary District sewage plant at Stickney, the farm still produces its crops and the the woods still afford adventure and mosquitoes.

While their ties to the land would suggest conservatism, the Nadelhoffers are no "American Gothic" pair. Herb is a high school teacher and Ph.D. candidate in Public Address and Group Communication at Northwestern University. Julie is a public health nurse trained at Yale who also teaches Russian as a sideline. Both are intense devotees of environmental literature and take an active role in the proselytizing of local public officials to the cause of ecology.

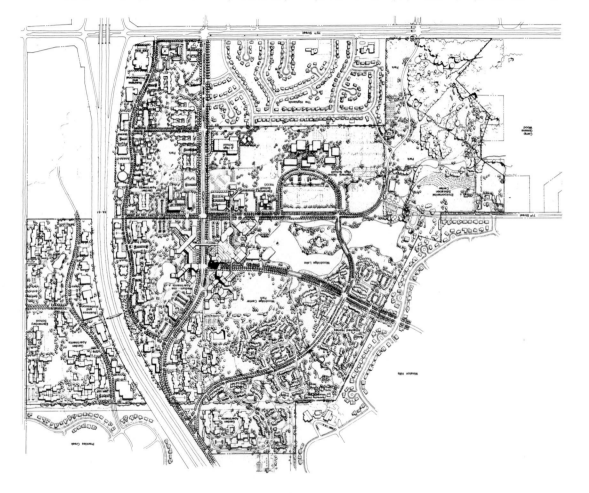

*Figure 22. Site Plan for "Woodridge Center," a Planned Unit Development proposal by Brown-Heldt Associates as consultants to the Woodridge Center Owners Group. Environmental Center is at lower left; park, lake, and high-rise Village Center are in middle of plan.*

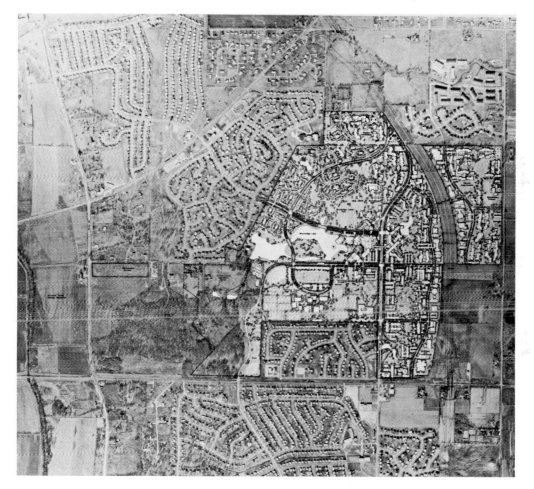

*Figure 23. The 60-acre Environmental Center as envisioned in the site plan for the Nadelhoffer farm and neighboring properties. Courtesy of Brown-Heldt Associates.*

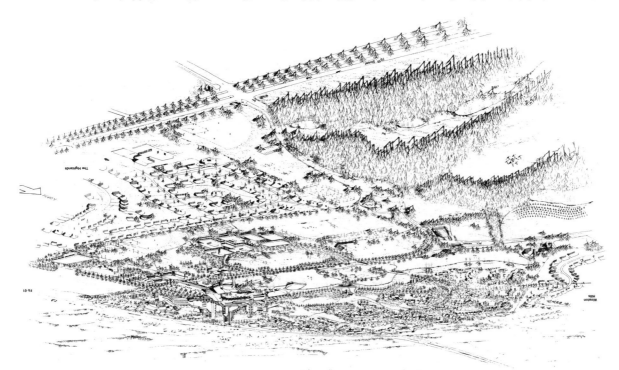

Figure 24.  Aerial view of the planned community of Woodridge Center. Courtesy of Brown-Heldt Associates.

The prospects for preserving their farm in its entirety being nil, the Nadelhoffers began to consider how development of the property might have landmark significance rather than producing another stamped-out subdivision. In particular, they wanted to preserve the woods and marsh as a place for study of the natural environment, as well as to include greenways and other open space features in the built-up portion of the development.

The Nadelhoffers soon realized that their best hope for influencing the course of development lay in maximizing the amount of land which they could offer as a package to a developer, who could thereby take advantage of economies of scale. Accordingly, they began to carry their cause to other owners of property in the vicinity, beginning with their own co-owners of the family farm. An important ally was Herb's brother Carleton, who consented after some persuasion to serve as legal counsel for the enterprise.

With the aid of maps they prepared themselves, a "land advocacy memo" from the Open Lands Project, and a variety of books and pamphlets on environmental planning, the Nadelhoffers contacted each of their "non-subdivision" neighbors. The surrounding large properties were a varied lot, consisting of two wooded estates, a mink ranch, a sod farm, and some agricultural land. All of the owners, pressed by taxes and aware of the imminent transition of the area, were intrigued by the proposition to pool their lands and procure a development of superior design.

An early threat to the viability of the project was a hefty offer to the owner of 30 acres of woods. Because the neighbor was anxious to sell, the loss of this property directly adjacent to the Nadelhoffer woods seemed inevitable. The threat was nipped when William B. Greene, a retired industrialist and philanthropist, stepped in to buy the property. Mr. Greene had previously established a forest preserve and a Girl Scout Camp in the vicinity through donations of land. His timely purchase of the tract served both to protect the scout property and to maintain the integrity of the Nadelhoffers' plan. Mr. Greene thus became a member of the land "pool."

To determine the practical feasibility of the idea, the Open Lands Project helped to arrange a series of meetings between the Woodridge neighbors and the Chicago-based development firm of Urban Associates. The officers of this firm, attorney Marshall M. Holleb and planner Ira J. Bach, were both enthusiastic about the concept, including its open space aspects. Holleb suggested that property owners could be offered a choice between being paid off in cash or accepting the status of limited partners to share in the planning and eventual profits of the enterprise. Preliminary conversations were complicated, however, by the large number and differing concerns of the property owners; no arrangement was immediately agreed upon.

Instead, the neighbors moved in a more self-deterministic direction. Having accepted the Nadelhoffers' thesis that power lay in the direction of cooperative action, they formed a provisional syndicate in which they agreed to keep their land off the market for a year and to contribute to the cost of landscape design study of the entire collective property.

To perform the study and plan, the Woodridge group turned to Thomas Brown, a nephew of William B. Greene and a former member of the firm of Lawrence Halprin Associates. Now a partner in Brown/Heldt Associates of San Francisco, Mr. Brown had grown up on a farm near the Nadelhoffers and was fully sympathetic with their philosophy regarding the land.

The package which the neighbors had assembled comprised about 480 acres, including upland fields, woods, and marsh. In addition to the village limits of Woodridge, the right of way for a future expressway bordered it to the east. Its western extremity bordered on the Girl Scout Camp, beyond which lay the extensive Greene Valley Forest Preserve.

Brown's plan was drawn to heighten the natural advantages and to diminish the manmade disadvantages of the site. In the former category, it provided for the preservation of the woods and marsh in a 60- to 80-acre "outdoor environmental center," as suggested originally by the Nadelhoffers. It proposed an artificial lake for recreation and scenic benefit in the manner of Reston, Virginia. Facing the lake and extending across the upland areas would be townhouses, garden apartments, and high rises containing some 5,000 units. These would be interspersed with "greenways" and a large recreational field.

In alleviation of Woodridge's present deficiency in commercial and cultural resources, the project envisions a major community center providing a focus for all village residents. Daring architecture and underground parking would contribute to the realization of a new style of suburban center, accessible by foot or electric vehicle. School facilities already under construction would be linked by pathways to a town library as well as to the environmental center.

The Brown/Heldt plan would, of course, entail planned unit development. It is currently being presented to Village officials and to the school, park, library, and other local boards for their consideration. At this writing, the Nadelhoffer group anticipate receiving approval of their PUD proposal in consideration for agreement to annex their unincorporated property to Woodridge. If such a pre-annexation agreement is reached, the group will be in an excellent position to select the best possible developer to carry out the project.

The Nadelhoffer "do it yourself" approach to land planning and development is not recommended for those who are squeamish about local politics or who wish to sell their land as fast as possible. Delay, frustrations, and financial costs in taxes and consultant fees are unavoidable. Local public officials may be unreceptive unless the plan clearly benefits the existing community as well as the residents of the proposed addition. Neighbors may be unable to find a basis for pooling their lands.

In the light of progress to date, however, the Woodridge case shows that such obstacles can be overcome, given the dual incentive of eventual financial return and a clear conscience.

# CONCLUSION

This book has attempted to provide a rough guide to the largely unexplored subject of private citizen action in the urban development process. Through case studies of actual experiences, together with conceptual analysis of the opportunities available, it is hoped that the reader may have been aroused from the lethargy of despair. Although not every land-saving effort succeeds, the exercise is stimulating!

The rewards of land advocacy are not usually economic ones. Although the preservation of open land may increase property values in the vicinity, such an uncertain increment scarcely seems equivalent to the investment of time, energy, and financial sacrifice which land advocacy often entails. It would seem that such behavior is anomalous to the classical economics standard of "the reasonable man." Perhaps we have uncovered a new urban norm: "the ecological man."

Land-saving efforts by persons other than the owner violate another "sacred cow" of land economics and law, namely, that the owner should have complete dominance over his property, subject only to limited governmental intervention. The notion that residents of the area may interfere with the use of land intended by the owner and officials of local government does not fall within any category of established legal right. For the first time, purchasers of land having significance for open space purposes should be on notice to expect citizen intervention in the speedy execution of their development plans.

The great park systems of Europe have often been the product of dictatorial control: Haussmann's Paris and Nash's London are the best known examples. United States metropolitan areas lack benevolent monarchs. Indeed, they lack any kind of centralized control at all. Public officials often have little understanding of the functions and benefits of open space, and those officials responsible for open space programs usually do not have adequate funds to carry their plans into execution.

In the face of all these deficiencies, only private initiative can ensure that the metropolitan habitat remains habitable.

## NOTES

1. Gertrude Stein, *The Geographical History of America: or the Relation of Human Nature to the Human Mind* (New York: Random House, 1936).

2. Urban Land Institute, "Future Growth of Major U. S. Urban Regions," *Urban Land* 26, no. 2 (Feb. 1967).

3. Outdoor Recreation Resources Review Commission, *Outdoor Recreation for America,* p. 35.

4. Edward Higbee, "Agricultural Land on the Urban Fringe," in *Metropolis on the Move,* Jean Gottman and Robert A. Harper, eds. (New York: John Wiley & Sons, 1967), p. 65.

5. William C. Wheaton, "Form and Structure of the Metropolitan Area," in *Environment for Man: The Next Fifty Years,* William R. Ewald, Jr., ed. (Bloomington & London: Indiana University Press, 1967), p. 172.

6. Proposed Bill on "Conservation Easements," Illinois Planning and Conservation League, 1970.

7. John J. B. Miller, *Open Land in Metropolitan Chicago* (Chicago: Midwest Open Land Association, 1962), figs. 2-4.

8. Northeastern Illinois Planning Commission, "Ten Year Report," 1967, p. 18.

9. "Population, Employment and Land Use Forecasts . . ." NIPC Planning Paper no. 10 (Chicago: Northeastern Illinois Planning Commission, 1969).

10. Herbert P. Read, "The Dunes—The Army—The Battle," *The Izaak Walton Magazine* (Feb. 1967), p. 10.

11. F. M. Fryxell, *The Physiography of Region of Chicago* (Chicago: The University of Chicago Press, 1927).

12. "Diversity Within Order," Northeastern Illinois Planning Commission, 1967, p. 25.

13. Miller, op. cit., p. 53.

14. *Chicago Tribune,* November 28, 1965.

15. *Blackstone's Commentaries* (1768), p. 137, quoted in Charles M. Haar, *Land Use Planning* (Boston: Little, Brown & Co., 1959), p. 410.

16. 16 *Corpus Juris Secondum,* sec. 174.

17. *Illinois Revised Statutes,* chap. 34, sec. 3151. Hereafter cited as *Ill. Rev. Stat.*

18. *Ill. Rev. Stat.,* chap. 24, sec. 11-13-1.

19. *Ill. Rev. Stat.,* chap. 24, sec. 7-1-1 *et seq.*

20. 33 *Municipal Law Journal* 3 (July 1968).

21. William G. Colman, "Revenue Sharing: Problems and Prospects," *The Urban Lawyer* 34 (Spring, 1969).

22. *Illinois Constitution,* art. 9, sec. 1.

23. Edward J. Kaiser, "Natural Landscape and Housing Location Decisions," *Landscape Architecture* (Jan. 1970), pp. 105-107.

24. *Internal Revenue Code* (1954), sec. 170(a)(1). Hereafter cited as *Int. Rev. Code.*

25. *Int. Rev. Code,* sec. 170(b)(1)(D)(i).

26. *Int. Rev. Code,* sec. 170(b)(1)(B).

27. *Int. Rev. Code,* sec. 170(b)(2).

28. *Revenue Ruling,* 68-655.

29. *Int. Rev. Code,* sec. 170(d)(1).

30. U. S. Treasury Regulations, sec. 1. 170-1(c) (1958).

31. William H. Whyte, *Cluster Development* (New York: American Conservation Association, 1964).

32. Charles Little, *Challenge of the Land* (New York: Open Space Action Institute), p. 65.

33. William H. Whyte, *The Last Landscape* (Garden City: Doubleday & Co., 1968), p. 103.

34. Ibid., p. 107.

35. William H. Whyte, *Securing Open Space for Urban America: Conservation Easements* (Washington, D. C.: Urban Land Institute, Technical Bulletin 36, 1959), p. 38.

36. George Fell, Illinois Nature Preserves Memo (June 17, 1969).

37. *Ill. Rev. Stat.,* chap. 127, sec. 63a9.

38. *Ill. Rev. Stat.,* chap. 57-1/2, sec. 112(d).

39. *Ill. Rev. Stat.,* chap. 105, sec. 466b.

40. *Revenue Ruling* 64-205; 1964-2, Cum. Bul. 62.

41. *Int. Rev. Code,* sec. 170(a)(3).

42. *Int. Rev. Code,* sec. 170(f)(3)(B)(i) (1969).

43. *Treasury Regulation* S1. 1001-1(e) (1957).

44. 75 Stat. 183, 42 U.S.C. 1500-1500e, as amended by Housing and Urban Development Act of 1965, Title IX, 79 Stat. 494 (1965).

45. State of Illinois, Department of Conservation *Annual Report,* 1967, p. 32.

46. Northeastern Illinois Metropolitan Area Planning Commission, *Open Space in Northeastern Illinois,* Technical Report no. 2 (1962), p. 13.

47. John E. Trotter, *State Park System in Illinois* (Chicago: University of Chicago Department of Geography, Research Paper no. 74, 1962), p. 72.

48. *Ill. Rev. Stat.,* chap. 105, sec. 465 (1963).

49. *Ill. Rev. Stat.,* chap. 57-1/2, sec. 6(a) (1965).

50. *Ill. Rev. Stat.,* chap. 57-1/2, sec. 5 (1967).

51. Northeastern Illinois Planning Commission, Population Forecasts, op. cit.

52. "Land Acquisition Master Plan for the DuPage County Forest Preserve District," mimeo, 1965.

53. "Land Purchase Plan Adopted," *The Chicago Tribune,* November 22, 1968.

54. Northeastern Illinois Planning Commission, Newsletter (Oct. 1969), p. 4.

55. *Ill. Rev. Stat.,* chap. 57-1/2, sec. 101 *et seq.* (1963).

56. *Outdoor Recreation in Illinois* (Springfield: Department of Business and Economic Development, 1965), p. 56.

57. Ibid.

58. *Ill. Rev. Stat.,* chap. 24, sec. 11-48. 2-1 *et seq.*

59. *Ill. Rev. Stat.,* chap. 32, sec. 163 (a) (1) *et seq.*

60. *Ill. Rev. Stat.,* chap. 70, sec. 31, *et seq.* (1965).

61. *Ill. Rev. Stat.,* chap. 32, sec. 163 (a) (1) *et seq.*

62. See, generally, George G. Bogert, *Handbook of the Law of Trusts* (St. Paul, Minn.: West Publishing Co., 1952).

63. Russell L. Brenneman, *Private Approaches to the Preservation of Open Land* (Washington: The Conservation and Research Foundation, 1967), p. 14.

64. Ibid., p. 19.

65. *Int. Rev. Code,* sec. 170 (b) (1) (D).

66. Linda A. Murray, *Land Trusts* (mimeo), Open Space Action Institute, 1968.

67. *Ill. Rev. Stat.,* chap. 30, sec. 153 (1963).

68. *Ill. Rev. Stat.,* chap. 83, sec. 12.1 *et seq.*

69. *Ill. Rev. Stat.,* chap. 20, sec. 37(b).

70. *Ill. Rev. Stat.,* chap. 30, sec. 37(c).

71. *Ill. Rev. Stat.,* chap. 30, sec. 37(d).

72. *Ill. Rev. Stat.,* chap. 30, sec. 37(e).

73. Allison Dunham, *Preservation of Open Space Areas* (Chicago: Midwest Open Lands Association, 1965).

74. Ibid., and 4 Restatement of Property, sec. 396 (1944).

75. Brenneman, op. cit., p. 9.

76. See, generally, Whyte, op. cit., note 31.

77. Carl Norcross, *Open Space Communities in the Market Place* (Washington, D.C.: Urban Land Institute, 1966).

## BIBLIOGRAPHY

Babcock, Richard F. *The Zoning Game.* Madison; University of Wisconsin Press, 1966.
>A practitioner's candid impressions of the idiosyncracies of zoning policy and procedure in the United States.

Brenneman, Russell L. *Private Approaches to the Preservation of Open Land.* The Conservation and Research Foundation, 1967.
>A well-documented lawyer's discussion of the ways and means of saving private open land. Describes experience in Connecticut.

Citizens Advisory Committee on Environmental Quality. *Community Action for Environmental Quality.* Washington, D.C.: U.S. Government Printing Office, 1967.
>A quick summary of the various tools available for better community planning.

Dunham, Allison. *Preservation of Open Space Areas.* Chicago Midwest Open Land Association, 1963.
>A law professor's study of the legal provisions relating to open space in Illinois, Indiana, Michigan, and Wisconsin; also describes how to set up a private open space agency.

Goodman, William I. *The Implementation of Public Programs of Open Space.* Bureau of Community Planning and Department of Urban Planning University of Illinois. Urbana: Mimeo, 1965.
>A scholar's inventory of the public role in open space preservation.

Herring, Francis W., ed. *Open Space and the Law.* Berkeley: Institute of Governmental Studies, University of California, Berkeley, 1965.
>A symposium on the state of the law relating to open space. Discusses recent developments in eminent domain, zoning and taxation.

Krasnowiecki, Jan. *Planned Unit Residential Development.* Urban Land Institute, Technical Bulletin No. 52. Washington: Urban Land Institute, 1965.
>A survey of constitutional and statutory provisions affecting P.U.D. approval.

Little, Charles E. *Challenge of the Land.* New York: Open Space Action Institute, 1968.
>A manual for local public officials and concerned citizens. Describes experience in New York, New Jersey and Connecticut. Includes sample ordinances.

Little, Charles E. *Stewardship.* New York: Open Space Action Committee, 1965.
>The original document on the subject. Describes examples of stewardship in the New York metropolitan area.

Siegal, Shirley Adelson. *The Law of Open Space*. New York: Regional Plan Association, 1960.
    A wide-ranging discussion of new legal theories and their applications relating to open space.
Strong, Ann Louise. *Preserving Urban Open Space*. Washington, D.C.: Urban Renewal Administration, 1963.
    A good short discussion of the basic concepts of open space preservation.
Whyte, William H. *The Last Landscape*. Garden City, N.Y.: Doubleday and Company, 1968.
    The authentic compilation of lore, strategy, theory, and common sense of open space preservation, in Whyte's entertaining style.
Whyte, William H. *Cluster Development*. New York: American Conservation Association, 1964.
    A monograph on the subject with an index of "open space communities" in existence.
Whyte, William H. *Securing Open Space for Urban America: Conservation Easements*. Urban Land Institute, Technical Bulletin No. 36. Washington, D.C.: Urban Land Institute, 1959.
Williams, Norman Jr. *Land Acquisition for Outdoor Recreation: Analysis of Selected Legal Problems*. Outdoor Recreation Resources Review Commission Study Report No. 16. Washington, D.C.: U.S. Government Printing Office, 1962.
    The legal volume of the famous ORRRC study.

## APPENDICES

Land advocacy is first and foremost a matter of communication, particularly through the written word. The writings related to land saving fall into two general categories, (1) formal legal instruments or legislative matter, and (2) informal persuasive writings. Other books, especially Charles Little's *Challenge of the Land,* contain specimens of formal documents. Model ordinances for the Chicago area may be obtained from the Northeastern Illinois Planning Commission, and any real property lawyer is familiar with the tools of his trade. This book therefore does not attempt to provide samples of such formal writings.

Informal persuasive writings, however, are in constant use by the Open Lands Project and by the citizen groups which it assists. It is felt that examples of these kinds of documents which are not set out elsewhere may prove to be useful to the reader. All except No. V were written by the author.

*Appendix I* is a fairly elaborate argument concerning the impending construction of a freeway through Thorn Creek Woods. It illustrates the kind of basic legal research which helps to bolster an otherwise a priori discussion of values and social objectives.

*Appendix II* is a constructive or promotional document which was widely circulated to the press and to private citizens in the upper Fox Valley with considerable response.

*Appendix III* is intended to warn and deter county officials from precipitous action on applications by large developers for massive rezoning of rural land to urban use.

*Appendix IV* is a copy of actual testimony which was made to a Forest Preserve District in the form of a prepared written statement. Persons delivering such a statement should normally have at least a dozen extra copies for the record, for the press, and for interested bystanders.

*Appendix V* illustrates a land advocate's "letter to the editor" of a suburban paper concerning a local land-saving opportunity (which was soon lost).

### APPENDIX I—Open Lands Project Advisory Memorandum, March 12, 1970

#### South Suburban Freeway Threatens Thorn Creek Woods

Efforts to preserve Thorn Creek Woods through public acquisition and private negotiation are foredoomed unless current plans of the Illinois Division of Highways, District Ten, to construct a freeway through the Woods are altered. Much of the value of the woods lies in its continuity and sense of removal from surrounding urbanization. To bi- or tri-sect this pocket wilderness with expressway lanes would render the remaining fragments practically useless for public preservation.

In its determination of a location for the South Suburban Freeway, the State Highway Department is confining its studies to the three mile wide "corridor" designated by the Chicago Area Transportation Study in 1962. The corridor is centered at this point on the Will-Cook County line. Since the Cook County portion is obstructed by the Village of Park Forest, study is being concentrated on the Will County half. Within this one and a half mile strip, five alternate alignments are under consideration. Since the woods lies athwart the corridor, as presently drawn, *all five of these alignments would invade Thorn Creek Woods*. The woods, however, could be entirely spared by locating the Freeway a mile to the south of the corridor.

#### Planners Committed to 1962 Corridor

The Division of Highways, however, is reluctant to consider any possible routes south of the 1962 corridor. According to Mr. Henry Yamanaka, an engineer with the Department, most of the demand for the road lies to the north; removal of the road southward would decrease its benefit to the communities of Chicago Heights, Park Forest, etc., which are inadequately served by Route 30. Special reliance is placed on the view of Barney Cunningham, President of the Village of Park Forest, who has stated that he wants the freeway as close as possible to Park Forest without actually passing through it. He adheres to this view despite its inconsistency with his stated position that Thorn Creek Woods should be saved. However, local residents believe that Cunningham's personal view concerning the freeway is not the official position of the Park Forest Board of Trustees. No vote has been taken on the matter.

While *existing* demand admittedly lies to the north of the County line, *future* demand will be largely generated in Will County, particularly if an airport is constructed there. *To quibble over a difference of a mile in north-south distance, therefore, is to plan for the past rather than the future.* Indeed, wherever the road is placed, new demand from industrial, commercial, and residential development will be thereby induced. This phenomenon is visible along all of the expressways and Tollways in the Chicago Metropolitan area.

### Need to Revise 1962 CATS Corridor

What is so sacred about the 1962 CATS corridor? The report from which it was derived stated:

This is not a plan of detailed locations—it is a system or network plan. Proposed new routes are shown diagrammatically—straight lines or sweeping curves. The plan could not pretend to be otherwise, since detailed planning is impossible without considering specific land uses, subsoils, acquisition costs, and without making structural and geometric engineering studies. . . .
As with any other plan, this one is subject to review and revision over the years . . . As Burnham wrote, "A diagram contains its own logic and tells its own story. If it is close to the truth, it will persist as a guide for future builders. If not, it will be revised as it passes through the various stages of review which come with time and political processes.' (Chicago Area Transportation Study, Vol. III, April 1962, p. 63.)

From its very inception, the 1962 corridor along the Will-Cook line was obviously a political compromise and a draftsman's convenience, not predicated upon actual population and desire-line data. It was never intended to be regarded as anything more than a gross estimate of approximate location.

Since the promulgation of this "diagram," the following changes have occurred in the vicinity of the corridor:

1. Incorporation and development of Park Forest South (scheduled population 30,000).
2. Planning of Governor's State University.
3. Possible construction of airport in Will County.
4. Growing recognition of the importance of Thorn Creek Woods as a recreational, conservation, and education-oriented regional open space.

All of these developments demand review and revision of the CATS 1962 corridor. *In fact, officials of the Governor's State University, the Village of Park Forest South, and Park Forest South Development Company have each urged that such revision be made and the Freeway be located south of the present corridor.* The conservation argument therefore is in harmony with the other major interests directly affected by the location of this Freeway.

Furthermore, costs of land acquisition and disruption of existing activity would be decreased, the farther south of the corridor the Freeway is located. Land values in Thorn Creek Woods are presently $2500-3500 and climbing rapidly. Will County farmland two miles south may be acquired at one third as much per acre.

### Needless Destruction of Woodlands for Highways Is Contrary to Federal Law

It is a matter of national policy that natural areas and open space in metropolitan regions be respected and preserved by federally aided activities. This policy has been most forcefully expressed in the National Environmental Policy Act of 1969:

### TITLE I

Declaration of a National Environmental Policy Sec. 101. (a) The Congress, recognizing the profound impact of man's activity on the interrelations of all components of

117

the natural environment, particularly the profound influences of population growth, high-density urbanization, industrial expansion, resource exploitation, and new and expanding technological advances and recognizing further the *critical importance of restoring and maintaining environmental quality* to the overall welfare and development of man, declares that it is the continuing policy of the Federal Government, in cooperation with State and local governments, and other concerned public and private organizations, to use all practicable means and measures, including financial and technical assistance, in a manner calculated to foster and promote the general welfare, *to create and maintain conditions under which man and nature can exist in productive harmony,* and fulfill the social economic, and other requirements of present and future generations of Americans. (emphasis added)

The Act calls upon the Federal Government to "use all practical means" to ensure that the Nation may: (1) fulfill the responsibilities of each generation as *trustee of the environment* for succeeding generations; (2) assure for all Americans safe, healthful, productive, and esthetically and culturally pleasing surroundings; . . . . (4) preserve important historic, cultural, and *natural aspects of our national , heritage.* . . . [emphasis added]

All agencies of the Federal Government are directed to

(C) include in every recommendation or report on proposals for legislation and other major Federal actions significantly affecting the quality of the human environment, a detailed statement by the responsible official on—(i) the environmental impact of the proposed action, (ii) any adverse environmental effects which cannot be avoided should the proposal be implemented, (iii) alternatives to the proposed action, (iv) the relationship between local short-term uses of man's environment and the maintenance and enhancement of long-term productivity, and (v) any irreversible and irretrievable commitments of resources which would be involved in the proposed action should it be implemented.

Consistent with the foregoing policy, the process of planning federally-aided highways is governed by the Department of Transportation Policy and Procedure Memorandum 20-8 (Jan. 14, 1969) whose purpose is to:

> [P]rovide a medium for free and open discussion . . . [and] to encourage early and amicable resolution of controversial issues that may arise.

The regulation requires in the case of new highways that a "corridor public hearing":

(1) [Be] held before the route location is approved and *before the State highway department is committed to a specific proposal;*

(2) [Be] held to ensure that an opportunity is afforded for effective participation by interested persons in the process of determining the need for and the location of, a Federal aid highway; and

(3) Provide a public forum that affords a full opportunity for presenting views on each of the proposed alternative highway locations and the social, economic, and *environmental effects* of those alternate locations.

### No Corridor Hearing Has Been Held Pertaining to the South Suburban Freeway

Aside from certain informal meetings with local interests, the Division of Highways has not yet held or scheduled a formal "corridor hearing." According to Mr. Yamanaka, such a hearing will be held upon the receipt of a study by the landscape architecture firm of Johnson, Johnson & Roy. Nevertheless, the engineering firm of C. F. Murphy Associates has already been retained to design the Freeway in accordance with one of the five alternative alignments *within* the 1962 CATS corridor. *This contract is evidence of "commitment to a specific proposal" on the part of the Division of Highways without having first held the required "corridor hearing."*

### APPENDIX II—Proposal for a "Fox Path": Elgin to Algoiquin

The Fox Valley between Elgin and the Chain O'Lakes is rapidly changing from an isolated region of farms, estates, and sleepy industrial villages into an unwilling extension of the Chicago Metropolitan Region. The opening of the Northwest Tollway, the migration of industries and business firms to the new complex at O'Hare, and the growth of businesses in the Fox Valley itself, all are causes of the development boom north of Elgin.

One of the swiftest transitions has been at Carpentersville which rose in population from 1,523 in 1950 to 17,424 in 1960 (including annexed territory). Local residents estimate that the 1969 population is about 27,000 with more building to come.

Many developments are in progress on the west side of the Fox. At Sleepy Hollow, West Dundee, Algonquin, and Cary, the bluffs overlooking the river are or soon will be sprouting with houses.

Local residents may cling to the hope that the Fox will remain rural despite the influx of thousands of urban dwellers. Reliance may be placed in large-lot zoning and faith that the newcomers will share the love of the river scenery that long-time residents have taken for granted.

Unfortunately, such assumptions only serve to feed inaction. *Nothing is* being done to *preserve the character of the Fox north of Elgin.*

Most deplorable is the lack of preserved wooded areas along the river. The public embankments at the Dundee and Algonquin are merely ornamental, not examples of river scenery or habitat. Neither the Dundee Township Park District nor the Kane County Forest Preserve District own a single acre on this stretch of the Fox.

Between towns and subdivisions, however, there still exist long stretches of uninterrupted river-side woods in private ownership. The normal river's edge is marked by a row of ancient willows and cottonwoods. Various species of oak dominate the uncleared portions of the floodplain. Ash, hickory, oak, and maple climb the bluffs.

A prize amenity of the Valley is its birdlife. Waterfowl such as ducks and geese nest where it is still wooded along the shore. Other bird life appears in profusion, no doubt augmented by the population reared in the McGraw Wildlife Preserve at Dundee. The Fox also is a flyway for migratory species.

While further inventory of the River's fast dwindling natural assets could be made, it is sufficient to say that action is needed:

1. To preserve that which remains of the natural river scenery and wildlife; and

2. To facilitate responsible public enjoyment of these amenities to the maximum extent consistent with their preservation.

The Open Lands Project has made a survey of the area under consideration, looking at both the physical character of the shorelines and the legal property interests involved. Without further elaboration at this time, we would make the following proposal:

1. Preservation and appreciation of the Fox River amenities may best be realized through establishment of a *public footpath* along the river's edge.

2. Such a footpath should be planned for either or both banks of the Fox between the northern limit of Elgin and the Kane-McHenry County line. (Extension southward to join the existing "Prairie Path" or northward into McHenry County would be logical future additions.)

3. Such a footpath should be strictly designed for non-motorized traffic, e.g., hiking, cycling, and perhaps riding, so as to minimize disturbance to wildlife and private property.

4. Establishment of a footpath may best be accomplished by a private not-for-profit association formed for the purpose, patterned on the Prairie Path and Green Bay Trail Associations.

5. Creation of the footpath would depend upon easements acquired through donation, purchase, necessity, or prescription. (Condemnation by public authority should be avoided.) Such easements would run from the property owner to the Association which would provide guarantees against liability and

6. Once established, the footpath would be conveyed to a suitable public authority such as the Kane Forest Preserve District or the Dundee Township Park District for permanent administration.

The creation of a footpath along the Fox would serve the two objectives listed above in the following way. By its very presence, it would serve as an effective deterrent to development directly at the river's edge. If backed up by "scenic easements," it could well be the backbone of a major open space system, *with scarcely any impact on existing private uses.*

If properly organized and publicized, a footpath would be of unlimited benefit to hikers and cyclists, in family, scout, school, church, or other organized groups. Residents of the immediate area, of course, would benefit most directly.

Many questions need to be asked in order for all the problems and opportunities represented by this proposal to be aired. Please contact me at the Open Lands Project if you are interested and would serve on a preliminary committee.

### APPENDIX III—Land Advocacy Memorandum, Ogle County, Lake Development Situation, August, 1970

#### Background

Ogle County, in Northwestern Illinois, is the fourth county west of Cook and the second east of the Mississippi River. One of the State's larger counties in area, Ogle has a population of only 42,000. Its principal towns are Oregon, the county seat, with 3800 people, Rochelle with 7500, Mount Morris, Forreston, Byron, Stillman Valley, and Polo. It has no east-west expressways, but Route 20 and the Northwest Tollway, which skirt Rockford a few miles to the north, provide access to the Chicago area in two hours.

Ogle is bisected by the Rock River, which flows through a scenic gorge near Oregon. Tributary creeks to the Rock have created a landscape of hills and ravines more interesting than the flat glacial outwash plains of DeKalb and LaSalle Counties. The County has two State Parks, White Pine Forest and Lowden, the latter being the site of Northern Illinois University's Lorado Taft Field Campus overlooking the Rock River.

The combination of easy access to a major population center and, for Illinois, unusually pleasant scenery, is attracting much interest from large developers seeking to reach the "second home" market. If present plans for seven separate developments (of which two have reached the stage of acquiring options on land) are carried to fruition, the county will double in population in the next ten years. The 1000 acre Lost Nation Lake development is already under construction in Taylor Township.

**Lake Developments**

The development concept which is proposed for Ogle County does not entail additions to existing towns or concentrations of large populations in genuine "new towns." Rather, as envisioned by the Branigar Organization and its competitors, the developments planned for Ogle have the following characteristics:

1. leisure-time atmosphere (recreation center and facilities for golf, tennis, etc.);
2. orientation to artificial lake;
3. medium density (2 to 4 lots per acre);
4. high priced lots;
5. exclusivity.

The ubiquitous feature in each development plan is an artificial lake to be created by damming one or more of the Rock tributaries. It is believed by the developers that water flow supplemented by wells if necessary would be sufficient to maintain such lakes at a constant level. As the most prominent feature of each community, the lake would afford fishing, swimming, and boating according to literature publicizing a similar development now underway at Apple Canyon Lake in Jo Daviess County. Such privileges would be limited to purchasers of lots and would not be available to the general public.

Public officials, bankers, lawyers, and merchants of Ogle County are ready to embrace the arriving developers in the belief that their "pot of gold" lies in store. According to the local newspaper: . . . The flow of millions of dollars may soon be headed toward the residents of Ogle County, as a result of a unique private lake development proposed for formation in Ogle

County. This huge influx of dollars would arrive in several forms, during and after the lake's development. Of foremost interest would be the tremendous increase in real estate tax income to Ogle County without a corresponding increase to the current landowners. . . .

"Of interest to local businessmen is the flow of hundreds of thousands of retail dollars spent, resulting from such a lake project." Mr. Harber [Vice President of the Branigar Organization] said. "At another of our developments called Lake Redstone, I can remember how the surrounding towns seemed to glow with prosperity". . . .

According to Harber, the predominant buyers of lake property are family people, wage earners and professional men. They appreciate the value of property, take care of it, support their local government and their church, and are an asset to a community.

"In a town near one of our lake developments," Harber related, "townfolk saw families who owned lake property coming to church on Sunday with the children or grandmother, perhaps, and this said a lot about their summertime neighbors." (*Republican-Reporter,* Nov. 20, 1969)

### Unresolved Issues

Some local residents, however, are taking a longer look at the implications of wholesale damming of natural watercourses and subdivision of farmland. In particular, they question the attitude of certain members of the County Board of Supervisors and the Board of Zoning Appeals whose enthusiasm for the blessings of development may conflict with the exercise of their critical judgment with respect to particular aspects of the proposed plans. (In one or two cases, it appears that members of the Zoning Board actually have land under option to a possible applicant for a zoning change.)

Basically, the critics of unlimited growth for growth's sake do not oppose development as such. They insist, however, that development must be socially responsible and in conformity with ecological reality. As apostles of Ian McHarg and William H. Whyte, they urge that Ogle County balance future social costs against short run profits in determining the actual merits of the proposed schemes.

Among the considerations which should be raised are:

1. *Sewage Disposal.* What will be the effect of massive residential development with

individual septic systems upon the watercourses and underground water sources of the County, not to mention upon the artificial lakes themselves?

2. *Flowage*. What will be the effect upon the Rock River of the damming of many of its tributaries? Will flowage levels be adequate to transport the load of effluent which the River is now required to receive, as well as added load from new sewage treatment plants in the future?

3. *Taxation*. Will the new developments pay their fair share of local taxes, including taxes on property retained by the development companies themselves? How will lake bottom real estate be taxed?

4. *Local Government*. Will the new communities be separately incorporated, be annexed to existing municipalities, or be administered under county government? Which is preferable for (a) the present residents of the county and (b) the future residents of the new communities?

5. *Schools*. What will be the school needs generated by the new developments? What does the developer propose to do towards meeting such needs? What does he expect of the present residents?

6. *Highways*. What will be the effect of the new population upon the county's highways and bridges? How will the developer contribute to the cost of improvements or new roads required by such increase in users?

7. *Open Space*. What will be the impact of the new leisure-oriented population upon the available supply of public open space, State Parks in particular? Will the developer dedicate land or contribute money to the public for the expansion of public parks and open space?

8. *Quality of Life*. Will Ogle County be a better or worse place to live in ten years as a result of the impending developments?

### APPENDIX IV—Statement of Open Lands Project to Will County Forest Preserve District Board of Commissioners

Gentlemen:

The Open Lands Project is a non-profit private conservation agency incorporated in the State of Illinois for the purpose of maintaining and improving the environment in which we live. Present today are 2 members of our Board of Directors: Dr. George Woodruff and Dr. Charles Samelson, and Mr. Rutherford Platt, our staff attorney.

Our statement will not reiterate what the Thorne Creek Preservation Association has already told you collectively and individually about Thorne Creek Woods. Many of you have seen the Woods and we believe there is no dispute by anyone that the area is a magnificent natural resource in its present state. If the land could be obtained for free, we doubt there is a man in the room who would say it should be torn apart for apartment houses and private commercial profit.

The real question, then, is whether public money should be spent for Thorne Creek Woods. We ask you in pondering this question to consider the various functions and benefits which the Woods would provide to the Will County of the future which justify its preservation today.

*First, Recreation.* Hiking and nature walking are among the fastest growing outdoor activities in northeastern Illinois according to the Illinois Recreation Plan 1967 Addendum. As a forest preserve, Thorne Creek Woods would afford much needed outdoor space for such activities in the midst of a heavily populated area. Moreover, as the biggest and best known forest preserve in Will County, Thorne Creek Woods would serve not only the immediate townships of Crete and Monee, but the entire County on a day-trip basis. Without Thorne Creek Woods, Will County will be sadly impoverished for outdoor recreation space.

*Second, Education.* The children living in the built-up parts of Will County are cut off from contact with nature in their daily lives. To compensate for this loss, Illinois law now requires that conservation education be included in school courses of study.

But understanding of nature cannot be learned only from books. Thorne Creek Woods with its variety of landforms and plantlife could be an excellent outdoor education center for Will County's schoolchildren. Classes would be brought there to see its woods, ponds, creeks, swamps, ravines, and meadows. With qualified teachers, they could begin to appreciate the importance of conservation and the natural basis of our man-made environment.

Such outdoor education centers are being created in other counties and by the Joliet Park

126

District. Will the schoolchildren in other parts of Will County be deprived of such an experience. (Is the Forest Preserve District too poor to meet the needs of the future?)

*Third, Hydrology.* Eleven floods have occurred during the past twenty-five years in the Thorne Creek Basin. Five of these have been in the last four years. As development adds more and more impervious surfaces in the form of roofs, roads, and parking lots, the run-off via Thorne Creek will be an ever more serious threat to property and life. If the water holding capacity of Thorne Creek Woods is stripped away, the flood problem will be even worse.

Furthermore, ground water acquifiers in northeast Will County depend in large measure upon Thorne Creek Woods as a natural recharge facility. Without the woods, the ground water table will be lower than ever and water shortages can be expected in many areas.

Therefore the Open Lands Project respectfully suggests that preservation of Thorne Creek Woods would serve at least three vital functions in Will County: *recreation, education,* and *hydrologic conservation.* With these benefits in mind, let us now face the costs involved.

No one maintains that Thorne Creek Woods can be obtained cheaply. Its owner is entitled to the fair market value of the land as required by Illinois law. According to a column in last Friday's *Chicago Sun-Times* based on information supplied by the owner, the land may be worth as much as $2000 an acre. True, this sounds like a lot for a county which still has lots of farm land. However, no more woods are likely to appear on the scene than there are now, and the price will never be less. DuPage County currently is paying on the average $10,800 per acre for its forest preserves; it simply waited too long to get started.

Will County is no longer just a rural downstate county. It has growing urban problems and has the resources with which to meet them. It has a tax roll of one billion dollars assessed valuation and a permissible bonding capability for forest preserves of five million dollars: the purchase of Thorne Creek Woods is within its grasp. Of the five forest preserve districts of northeastern Illinois, Will is the only one that has issued no bonds. It is time to get on the "bondwagon"!

We do not expect you to "go it alone". The Open Lands Project is in close touch with the State Department of Conservation, the Department of Housing and Urban Development, and the Bureau of Outdoor Recreation. We pledge to do all we can to help you obtain assistance from one or more of these sources. In addition, the staff of the Northeast Illinois Planning Commission is actively interested in preserving the Woods and their technical assistance should be available in applying for a federal open space grant.

In order to procure outside assistance, however, the Will County Forest Preserve District must take the first initiative. By issuing bonds adequate to purchase at least part of the Woods, your good intentions will be demonstrated. Since Will County will enjoy most of the benefits of preserving Thorne Creek Woods, it is only reasonable that it should accept a principal share of the necessary public burden. If you take this step, the future residents of Will County will praise your foresight—if you don't they may never forgive you.

### APPENDIX V—Letter to the Editor

To the Editor:

Yours is a newspaper with a refreshing sense of "the environment"—and while maybe ours in this town is not as depressed as elsewhere, I have become personally outraged by a hidden piece of environmental news that lately emerged somewhat by accident. I hope you get interested and outraged too.

It has to do with another form of commercialization on the west side that will destroy the final vestige of a mature forest tract. It must be between [10 and 12 acres].

This long-growing woodland begins at the Wilson-Jump store at Clavey and Skokie and runs a thousand feet south. It also is very deep, from the highway west to the railroad. It harbors a tremendous variety of birds, trees and plants (even wild strawberries). Flooding is reduced, and oxygen is produced, because it's there.

But apparently because there are a couple of automobile agencies in the neighborhood, somebody here, or in Detroit, or both, thinks the acreage is a fine place for another auto showroom.

So, very quietly, the Chrysler Corp. has acquired the property; and according to the building industry's construction-bid newspaper, is looking for somebody to bulldoze the woods, pave it all and put up a half-million dollar building.

This is the plan nobody knows about. This is the way important natural areas are here to benefit us one day—but gone the next. The people who do these jobs never, themselves, even seem to think of their total lives . . . only their short-term profit lives. It is incredible.

Industrial and commercial growth in this suburb (and any other) may have been a good idea in the good old days when the town was undeveloped. Now, though, it's become very rapidly overdeveloped—so much so that neither the citizens nor its part-time councilmen and administrators seem to know what's happening before it happens. Time never remains for thinking and study.

Obviously, from all the "environmental headlines" in all the papers now, commerce can't have first-say-so over our lands. Nobody can afford that philosophy any more. We're all ready to choke in Highland Park from what we already have, so how can anybody think there's any wisdom in accelerating development?

Along with the other open space areas in Skokie Valley, east of the highway, this small woodland is very close to all that we have left . . . all of which nobody is doing very much about. There is no "automatic forest-preserve district" which does these kinds of the jobs for "future generations" . . . like in the good old days. Now, only us folks—with or without the direct or indirect assistance of the town government—can do the saving.

I hope those who read this will feel the same sort of outrage that I do, and will understand that they are being informed in advance (although maybe only by 30 days) so that they can try to make a movement to save this woodland—as I am trying to do with this letter.

If you know anybody connected with an organization called "Three's Chrysler Plymouth," you could start with them, and try to convince them it's a bad idea to continue fouling our environment by insisting on destroying a beautiful wooded tract. There are other already-fouled tracts on Skokie which ought to be equally suitable—that is, if downtown Highland Park just absolutely isn't good enough anymore for displaying new and used cars.

129

If we can get a "moratorium" on this woods, then it ought to be possible to find ways to bring it into the open-space program which even the Federal government supports with special funds.

I am doing everything I can think of, including writing and telephoning anybody who can advise or help, including writing the president of Chrysler. If you want to help, you're welcome to telephone me any day except Thursday and Sunday at my office, 831-3430.

My office, incidentally, happens to be right next door to this living forest. Therefore I've watched and enjoyed it a long time. Therefore I am especially aware of the fact that when it's gone, it's all gone. Our lives will be poorer.—D. William Bennett, *Highland Park Life* newspaper, May 21, 1970.

# INDEX